THE PSYCHOLOGY OF TRAVEL

Why do we travel? Are holidays good for our health? What are the social and psychological factors that drive us to move?

The Psychology of Travel provides an eclectic introduction to the range of travel experiences from commuting, to going on holiday, to studying abroad. Travel is a near-universal experience and manifests itself in various forms, from everyday experiences to exotic adventure, although it varies across time and cultures. This book unpacks the concept of travel, and engages with topics including migration, wellbeing, acculturation, wayfinding, slow travel, place attachment and nostalgia, and brings them into sharp focus in relation to globalisation and climate change.

By offering key insights into the psychological factors behind different kinds of travel, The Psychology of Travel introduces the reader to new ways of thinking about global mobility and movement.

Andrew Stevenson is a Senior Lecturer in Psychology at Manchester Metropolitan University. He is a Cultural Psychologist, with a particular interested in Social and Visual Anthropology and Cultural Geography, which he has explored through ethnographic documentary films and soundscapes. He is the author of Cultural Issues in Psychology (Routledge, 2020).

THE PSYCHOLOGY OF EVERYTHING

People are fascinated by psychology, and what makes humans tick. Why do we think and behave the way we do? We've all met armchair psychologists claiming to have the answers, and people that ask if psychologists can tell what they're thinking. The Psychology of Everything is a series of books which debunk the popular myths and pseudo-science surrounding some of life's biggest questions.

The series explores the hidden psychological factors that drive us, from our subconscious desires and aversions, to our natural social instincts. Absorbing, informative, and always intriguing, each book is written by an expert in the field, examining how research-based knowledge compares with popular wisdom, and showing how psychology can truly enrich our understanding of modern life.

Applying a psychological lens to an array of topics and contemporary concerns – from sex, to fashion, to conspiracy theories – The Psychology of Everything will make you look at everything in a new way.

Titles in the series

The Psychology of Exercise
by Josephine Perry

The Psychology of Wellness
by Gary W. Wood

The Psychology of Video Games
by Celia Hodent

The Psychology of Comedy
by G Neil Martin

The Psychology of Religion
by Vassilis Saroglou

The Psychology of Democracy
by Darren G. Lilleker and Billur Aslan Ozgul

The Psychology of Belonging
by Kelly-Ann Allen

The Psychology of Everything
by Marie Percival

The Psychology of Art
by George Mather

The Psychology of Travel
by Andrew Stevenson

For further information about this series please visit www. routledgetextbooks.com/textbooks/thepsychologyofeverything/

THE PSYCHOLOGY
OF TRAVEL

ANDREW STEVENSON

Routledge
Taylor & Francis Group

LONDON AND NEW YORK

Cover image: © Getty Images

First published 2023
by Routledge
4 Park Square, Milton Park, Abingdon, Oxon OX14 4RN

and by Routledge
605 Third Avenue, New York, NY 10158

Routledge is an imprint of the Taylor & Francis Group, an informa business

© 2023 Andrew Stevenson

British Library Cataloguing-in-Publication Data
A catalogue record for this book is available from the British Library

Library of Congress Cataloging-in-Publication Data
A catalog record for this book has been requested

ISBN: 978-1-032-10484-3 (hbk)
ISBN: 978-1-032-10479-9 (pbk)
ISBN: 978-1-003-21553-0 (ebk)

DOI: 10.4324/9781003215530

Typeset in Joanna
by Apex CoVantage, LLC

CONTENTS

1   Departure: towards a psychology of travel   1

2   Directions of travel: cognition, wayfinding
    and how to avoid getting lost   7

3   Influencers and trip advisors: the social
    psychology of travel   21

4   Travel fever: a worrying world of fear, phobia
    and anxiety   35

5   Hedonism and self-improvement: how does
    travel make us happier?   49

6   Unforgettable journeys: nostalgia, homesickness
    and other travel memories   63

7   Culture shocks and border crossings: travel
    and intercultural encounter   77

8   Detour: psychogeography and the art of slow travel   93

9   Where do we go from here? Travel in an age
     of eco-anxiety   109

Further reading   121
References   125
Index   149

1

DEPARTURE: TOWARDS A PSYCHOLOGY OF TRAVEL

WHAT'S THE DIFFERENCE BETWEEN MOBILITY, TRAVEL AND TOURISM?

Being in transit is a relatively normal state for many people. Mobility and travel contribute so much to the range of human experience that places of transition like streets, airports, footpaths, canals and railway stations can become as familiar as the destinations they lead to. Whether commuting to work, visiting friends in another part of the country, or crossing international borders for pleasure, work or worship, we spend much of our time on the way to somewhere else. The terms mobility, travel and tourism are often used interchangeably. But how are they different from each other? We use the term mobility to refer to all forms of movement, including mundane, repetitive journeys, like going to the shops or commuting to work. We usually refer to less repetitive, longer journeys as travel. After all, if someone says they are going travelling we are unlikely to picture them taking the bus to work or roaming their neighbourhood streets.

If travel is a subset of mobility, tourism is a subset of travel. Although all tourism involves some aspect of travel, not all travel is tourism. Novelist Paul Bowles (2000) distinguishes between tourism and travel thus

> Whereas the tourist generally hurries back home at the end of a
> few weeks or months, the traveller belongs no more to one place

DOI: 10.4324/9781003215530-1

than to the next, moves slowly over periods of years, from one part of the earth to another.

Bowles (2000), *The Sheltering Sky*

The difference between travel and tourism has long been debated, sometimes to the point of absurdity. In 1973, the National Tourism Resources Review Commission defined a tourist as someone travelling for a minimum of 50 miles for business, pleasure, personal affairs or any purpose other than commuting to work. Others have suggested that tourism includes any journey from place to place, excluding trips made for necessary, everyday activities, like shopping (Hunt & Layne, 1991). In 1975, hedging their bets slightly, the extravagantly named Tourism Research Planning Committee of the Federal Provincial Conference on Tourism in Canada defined a traveller as 'any person who travels' (Hunt & Layne, 1991). More helpfully, we can regard tourism as the temporary, short-term movement to relatively novel destinations, incorporating the activities undertaken at these destinations (Dilek & Dilek, 2018). In other words, tourism involves participating in a global industry, a social, cultural and economic phenomenon involving the movement of people for personal or pleasurable purposes, often in huge groups. Travel, on the other hand, denotes movement between locations for wider-ranging reasons, like leisure, recreation, spirituality, work, safety, study or health (Hall & Page, 2014). Tourism is also more likely to involve a return trip, whilst traveling may be more circuitous. Even if the two are hard to distinguish with the naked eye, for the sake of convenience we might agree that 'tourist' is a term more likely to be used by an observer. Meanwhile, a person in motion might prefer to be regarded as a 'traveller'.

Precise definitions aside, we can agree that travel is undertaken for various purposes, including education (boarding school, international study), religion (pilgrimage), employment (working abroad), leisure (tourism), health (convalescence), safety (refuge) or in pursuit of hedonistic, bodily pleasure (tourism again) (Cook, 2018). In 2015, 53% of international travel was for holiday or recreation, 14% was work-related and 27% for family visits, religious or health reasons (UNWTO, 2016). Travel (including tourism) is also a highly meaningful activity, amounting to much more than merely moving from A to B. Very often it is anticipated with a high level of excitement. It can leave us with long-lasting memories, fears, emotions and insights about who we are and how the world is (Cook, 2018). Besides broadening the mind, travel is also a social activity. After all, even when attempting to travel alone, chances are you will be surrounded by hundreds of people, and it may be that the opportunity to spend time with the exotic other is part of the attraction of travel in the first place. Who doesn't enjoy people watching? Travel is also unequally distributed globally. In 2021, 67.2% of international arrivals were in Europe, 19.3% were in the Americas (13% in the U.S.), 4.8% were in Asia and the Pacific, 4.3% in the Middle East, 1.4% in North Africa, and 2.9% to Sub-Saharan Africa (UNWTO, 2022). Meanwhile 48% of outbound international trips were from Europe in 2018, with 26% from Asia and the Pacific, 17% from the Americas, 3% from the Middle East. China, the U.S., Germany and the UK led the way as the four countries with the greatest spend on tourism (UNWTO, 2018). For many countries, like Tuvalu, Chad, Niger and Angola, outbound travel is far less common. Travel may be meaningful, memorable and exciting, but it is far from universally experienced.

Traditionally, travel research has been the domain of anthropologists and geographers (Cook, 2018). However, the experience of being on a journey undoubtedly raises interesting questions for psychologists too, because of its highly social, memorable, emotional and meaningful nature. Psychologists are also interested in travel because it is a complex cognitive activity that requires plenty of planning and problem-solving. As we will learn in subsequent chapters, psychological research has focused on questions about travel habits, motivations for travel, decision-making, emotional responses and satisfaction levels, as well as on how travel experiences relate to our sense of identity. After all, travel is fascinating because it leaves its mark on us and changes how we perceive ourselves and the places we visit. The aim of this volume is to bring together under one roof –

perhaps uniquely – responses to a range of travel-related questions that psychologists have pondered. Since movement is a state which so many people live with on a daily basis, arguably a psychology of travel is long overdue.

THE WAY AHEAD

Each subsequent chapter will focus on a distinct aspect of travel psychology.

Chapter 2, "Directions of travel: Cognition, wayfinding and how to avoid getting lost", explores the way travellers orientate themselves when arriving in a newly experienced place. This will strike a chord with anyone who has felt disorientated in a seemingly bewildering city or novel landscape. Arriving and wayfinding is a cognitive, social and corporeal process that involves the intellect, body and senses. It sometimes requires the help and guidance of other people too. This chapter will explore research into cognitive, sensorial and embodied approaches to arrival and wayfinding.

Chapter 3, "Influencers and trip advisors: The social psychology of travel", centres on the experience of traveling with other people, voluntarily or otherwise. Travel is a social activity and decisions about where and how to travel are open to social influence. Conformity effects, group membership and stereotypes about outsiders can all influence our experiences and choices relating to travel and tourism. We are also increasingly swayed in our decision-making when we use social media to help us plan journeys. This review of the social psychology of travel also looks at traveller typologies, and how different varieties of travellers engage with places differently. It also asks whether experiencing diverse locations can reduce prejudice against out-groups.

Chapter 4, "Travel fever: A worrying world of fear, phobia and anxiety", unpacks the historical case of travel fever. It also looks at more contemporary anxieties associated with flying, pathological fears of encountering new places, as well as the many sources of travel-related worry. Leaving your comfort zone behind can be both unsettling and stimulating, and to help those who experience anxiety at the thought of visiting new cultures or getting on an aeroplane, this chapter also reviews some techniques for reducing travel fever.

Chapter 5, "Hedonism and self-improvement: how does travel make us happier?", investigates the health benefits of travel and tourism. We discover some of the varieties of wellbeing that travel affords, ranging from the instant gratification of hedonistic pleasure to the more elevated, so-called eudemonic forms of self-improvement that travel can afford, such as learning a new language. Humanistic theories of flow and mindfulness are also considered in relation to how we can maximize the benefits of travel by living in the moment.

Chapter 6, "Unforgettable journeys: nostalgia, homesickness and other travel memories", looks at the nuanced relationship between travel and memory. Travel and migration can leave us with fond memories of the places we leave behind, often experienced as homesickness and nostalgia. But how are these different from each other? More positively, memories of home can also be used to help travellers make sense of newly encountered places. This chapter also explores the way the body and the senses help us to remember places we have previously visited. It also asks whether revisiting places can help to improve our memory capacity, especially with the help of technologies such as travel photography.

Chapter 7, "Culture shocks and border crossings: travel and intercultural encounter", focuses on the experience of travel for the purposes of long-term relocation. Migration presents anyone who moves to another country for work or study with intercultural encounters that can transform identities. These encounters require adaptations to behaviours, feelings and attitudes, including learning new norms in relation to language, food, dress habits and beliefs. To make sense of these transformations, cultural psychologists have developed theories of acculturation (adaptations made when moving from one culture to another), biculturalism (developing a dual identity after living in more than one culture) and cosmopolitanism (becoming fluent in several cultures). Each of these theories will be reviewed here.

In a slight departure, Chapter 8, "Detour: psychogeography and the art of slow travel", introduces the unique perspective of an interdisciplinary movement that combines art, psychology and geography. Psychogeography challenges us to make creative responses to the landscapes we move through, yielding artworks that constitute a dissenting voice in the psychology of travel, using writing, photography and other media. Located on the periphery of mainstream psychology, psychogeography is a playful detour into theories of mobility and creativity that critically question the way we experience and consume places we move through.

Finally, Chapter 9, "Where do we go from here? Travel in an age of anxiety", discusses contemporary debates about the psychology of travel in the era of global climate change and health emergencies. Answers to questions about how and where we travel are being revised in the wake of these global health, economic and climate emergencies. This chapter looks at the anxieties that arise from these revisions, using theories of digital nomadism and eco-anxiety to help us understand the psychological implications of traveling in uncertain times.

Have a good journey.

2

DIRECTIONS OF TRAVEL: COGNITION, WAYFINDING AND HOW TO AVOID GETTING LOST

ARRIVING AND NAVIGATING: AN INTRODUCTION TO WAYFINDING

Arriving in a place for the first time elicits feelings of excitement, expectation, curiosity, even trepidation. Whether we feel positive or negative about a place, getting there for the first time is an unrepeatable experience. Subsequent visits are likely to be less exciting. The positive thrill of arriving in an exotic location has even been reported by social scientists who travel to conduct research (Chang, 2013). In her essay "Fieldwork In Common Places", Mary Pratt (1992) reviews some notable (and poetic) arrival stories from the research archive. Arriving in Polynesia, Raymond Firth opens *We, The Tikopia* (1936) with these first impressions

> In the cool of the early morning, just before sunrise, the bow of the Southern Cross headed towards the eastern horizon, on which a tiny dark blue outline was faintly visible.
>
> (1936: 1)

Bronislaw Malinowski (1961) describes his first sight of the Trobriand Islands thus

DOI: 10.4324/9781003215530-2

Imagine yourself suddenly set down surrounded by your gear, alone on a tropical beach close to a native village while the launch or dinghy, which has brought you, sails away out of sight.

(1961: 4)

Arriving somewhere new can be disorientating, but it is what happens afterwards which has interested psychologists most: the considerable challenge of making sense of a new place. The psychology of negotiating routes around novel places has been researched using the term wayfinding (Xia et al., 2008). Research into wayfinding has been conducted in relation to encountering cities for the first time, negotiating labyrinthine airports, hospitals and workplaces.

Although a relatively recent arrival to psychology, wayfinding is not a new phenomenon. Sixteenth-century Polynesian Islanders used the stars for wayfinding, and island navigators were so esteemed for their abilities as to be awarded an elevated position in society (Gladwin, 1974). Psychologists have mainly regarded wayfinding as a cognitive process; an ability to find a route from A to B and execute it effectively (Xia et al., 2008). No doubt wayfinding is a handy skill for tourists, migrants, wanderers and others who travel.

There are varieties of wayfinding, just as there are varieties of travel (Allen, 1999). Commuter wayfinding is a daily, regular, repetitive process, undertaken in familiar surroundings, often centred on getting to work. Exploratory wayfinding, like taking a meandering walk, starts and ends in a familiar place, with much wandering in between. Quest wayfinding, the most adventurous variety, involves traveling into the unknown, perhaps across international borders, and finding one's way around an unfamiliar environment over a long period. We can also distinguish between recreational (leisurely and without time limit), resolute (a no-nonsense means of finding your way in the most efficient time available) and emergency (on a need-to-get-there basis, such as trying to make a travel connection) wayfinding (Fewings, 2001). In some travel scenarios, all three of these might be combined during different parts of a journey. Beyond this typology, we may find that as we incrementally come to know a new place, we pass through stages of wayfinding. The first of these, orientation, involves locating oneself in space. The second, route selection, involves choosing appropriate routes. Thirdly, route control, sees us sticking to effective routes. Fourthly, arrival, relates to knowing we have reached the required destination (Downs & Stea, 1973).

All these categories of wayfinding demonstrate its importance for travel psychologists. For travellers too, wayfinding matters because smooth passage enhances travel experience. Feelings of disorientation in a newly encountered place can provoke anxiety (Chang, 2013). Wayfinding research explores ways in which people with diverse abilities, in diverse locations, use cognition, embodiment and the senses to orient themselves. It has been studied across several travel contexts, from tourism, the workplace, to finding one's way through airports and healthcare facilities (Pati et al., 2015). Failures in wayfinding (aka getting lost) have been associated with high blood pressure, aggression and fatigue (Carpman & Grant, 2016), especially for older people and for those with impaired vision or mobility (Jamshidi & Pati, 2021). Wayfinding research matters because it informs environmental design, helps establish effective flows of people through bottlenecks and built environments and sheds light on experiences of travelers with different abilities, experiences levels and cultural backgrounds (Farr et al., 2014).

Kevin Lynch's book, The Image of the City (1960), is a milestone of wayfinding literature. A former architect, Lynch recognised the importance of wayfinding as an interaction between humans and built environments. He identified environmental elements that influence our ability to navigate. These include edges (paths, borders, walls), nodes (junctions) and landmarks (buildings, towers, statues). These environmental affordances facilitate successful route-making and navigation. They create legible environments that we can read while we are on the move. Besides environmental cues we use technologies (phones, maps, signs) to help us along our way, enabling us to visualise connections and distances between locations. Lynch deployed the terms legibility and imageability to describe the process by which we learn and recognise environmental patterns, effectively reading our surroundings. In doing so, he argued we use inner maps to interpret information and guide action.

Following Lynch's pioneering work the psychology of wayfinding has continued to explore how travellers understand and respond to new places, and how they adapt to them by developing their geographic literacy (Turner & Leydon, 2012). As we find our way, we develop an ability to read places using geospatial information and environmental cues and features by map reading, sensing direction, understanding travel signs and visualising routes and points between locations. Hence, we can reduce feelings of travel anxiety and enjoy the journey more (Chang et al., 2019). Failures in wayfinding don't just affect quality of experience. They can endanger life, or at least seriously disrupt travel.

Successful wayfinding depends on a combination of well-designed environments and individual abilities. It is an interplay between aptitudes (strengths, weaknesses, technological ability) and the way the environment has been designed, made legible with signage, lighting and so forth. Whilst recognising this interaction between individuals and environments, the psychology of wayfinding has been most closely associated with cognitive approaches; specifically, the concept of cognitive mapping.

THINKING ON YOUR FEET: COGNITIVE MAPPING

Finding your way around somewhere for the first time is an exercise in problem-solving. It involves navigating from an origin point (like an airport) to a destination (a hotel) (Lin et al., 2012). Cognitive psychologists have studied this process using a computer metaphor of a human information-processor. Environmental data is received and processed by the traveller in a goal-directed way. We constantly try to solve wayfinding problems using memory, attention and decision-making (Newell & Simon, 1972). We rely on a combination of pre-existing, internal cognitions and our ever-changing perceptions of the environment as we travel through it. According to Gibson's direct perception principle (1966), the environment provides our senses with all we need for effective perception. Thus, during way-finding, we use cues (or affordances) like angles, lines, signs, perspective, light and texture to help us to navigate adequately from A to B. On the other hand, Gregory (1980) stresses the need for prior cognitive processing (to supplement environmental data) to enable problem-solving and wayfinding. Hence, we need not just sensory information, but also prior memories, schemas, even internal maps.

The use of internal, cognitive maps is a wayfinding strategy which has been suggested as a means of helping us make sense of environmental cues (Kitchin & Blades, 2002). A cognitive map is an "internal representation of environmental information" (Tolman, 1948: 2). It is used to organise spatial cues and make decisions about route choices and wayfinding. The idea was suggested by behaviourist pioneer Edward Tolman (1948), whose maze rats responded to laboratory landmarks to help them learn routes. Subsequent research with humans focused on learning routes around cities and university campuses. As we move through landscapes, we accumulate internal representations which help us to make future navigation decisions. We do this iteratively, and how well we do it is influenced by travel mode and terrain. Cognitive mapping is a gradual, adaptive process through which we learn layouts and commit them to memory, often through mundane, repetitive experience. As active decision makers we move through streets, tree-lined pathways and corridors using environmental data for decision making, developing anticipatory schemas and hypotheses to guide future travel (Neisser, 1967).

The skill of cognitive mapping thrives on environmental exploration, beginning in infancy. The development of spatial knowledge in young children depends on small scale exploration (around nurseries, dwellings and neighbourhoods). Child development theory helps us understand the origins of wayfinding in relation to suggested stages of spatial ability. During these developmental stages, infants go from having a general sense of direction and place recognition, to a subsequent stage of recalling routes by using bodily memory, to finally being able to recognise and describe landmarks and their locations relative to one another (Mark & Frank, 1991). Passage through these stages, along with the construction of internal cognitive maps, depends on physical engagement with environments. This process is replicated on a larger scale in adulthood as we arrive in and explore new environments.

Like all maps, cognitive maps are open to distortion and idiosyncrasy (Kitchin & Blades, 2002). They are error-prone, personal representations rather than photographic memories (Golledge, 2002). Cognitive mapmaking uses anchor points (landmarks, road junctions) to help us form often unreliable internal maps (Gärling & Golledge, 2000). For example, it has been found that greater physical effort or repetition leads to more detailed maps. Distances between locations are exaggerated where travel is effortful, when there are hills or barriers (main roads, rivers) (Golledge, 2002). Cluttered or densely populated (with buildings and people) distances are also typically overestimated, as are those that are familiar (Kitchin & Blades, 2002). How we feel about a place also affects our internal representations. Places we like or feel attached to are judged to be closer than they really are. Some landmarks are recalled more readily if they have a positive emotional connotation. Desirable places are typically judged as closer than those that are undesirable (Ruotolo et al., 2018).

Cognitive mapping theory enlightens us about how we perceive and estimate distances in landscapes. Arguably though, the use of such internal representations tells us little about how groups of people with different strengths and challenges experience environments differently. It also has little to say about social wayfinding, which is especially relevant for those who travel with or amongst others. Arguably, wayfinding can be explored equally well by refocusing our attention from internal cognitive representations to the senses, the body and the social world (Symonds et al., 2017).

THE WISDOM OF CROWDS: SOCIAL WAYFINDING

Social wayfinding happens whilst travelling with and amongst other people. We usually travel amongst companions, crowds or bystanders. To illustrate this, Hutchins (2008) uses the example of navigating a ship's course, which is very much a collective enterprise; an example par excellence of human problem-solving and navigation as a social practice. Decisions at sea arise from back-and-forth communication between sailors in specific posts, using protocols and technologies to inform their decisions. This entourage method illustrates so-called distributed cognition (Hutchins, 2008); thought taking place between people and gadgets, rather than individually or internally. Whether at sea or on land, travel decisions are part of social wayfinding, where the presence of others, now or in the past, impact wayfinding and cognition (Dalton et al., 2019).

An obvious example is when two or more people plan and execute a route together. As you may know from experience, one person often dominates decisions in this dynamic, with others taking a back seat. Another manifestation of social wayfinding (even for lone travellers) is the mere presence of other people. We may see others on a path and consider it too busy (avoid it), or we may consider it to be safe (follow it). In travel, as in life, social influence and conformity affect our decisions.

We can distinguish between strong and weak social wayfinding (Dalton et al., 2019). In the strong version, other people communicate intentionally whilst co-navigating routes. This usually involves direct communication with someone in close proximity as part of an ongoing interaction, such as two people arriving in and navigating a city for the first time. This may be done synchronously, when messages are sent and received by travellers who are in the same place at the same time, for example walking along and talking. Alternatively, if protagonists are not physically together, they may pass messages remotely (texting or phoning) or follow instructions that have been previously sent (asynchronous). In strong social wayfinding (synchronous or asynchronous), decision-making is likely to be unequally distributed. For example, the person who is more familiar with the route may assume the leader role. Where both are equally familiar with the environment, mutual decision making is more likely (Gartner & Huang, 2012).

Another influential factor in strong social wayfinding is the relative senses of direction of the pair or group members. He et al. (2015) studied pairs with differing senses of direction navigating urban areas using mobile phones. We might assume in this scenario that when someone with a good sense of direction works with someone with a poor one, the former would prevail. Not necessarily so. A confounding factor in this assumption is metacognition; how good you think your sense of direction is. In separating the confident from the correct, (your belief about your sense of direction from your sense of direction itself), Bonner & Bolinger (2013) highlight the crucial difference between being the most knowledgeable person and thinking you are the most knowledgeable. A confident, less knowledgeable wayfinder may turn out to be an ineffective, even dangerous, travel partner. Forlizzi et al. (2010) supported this conclusion in research with co-navigators during car journeys.

Besides familiarity and metacognition, a third quality we might look for in a travel partner is social mindfulness (Van Doesum et al., 2013). When travelling in pairs, some people are better equipped psychologically to collaborate in wayfinding decisions (to put it politely). To put it bluntly, some co-travellers just don't listen. The model partner is one who is prepared to appreciate companions' preferences and perspectives, and to recognise their own influence on others. This is known as social mindfulness (Van Doesum et al., 2013). Mindfulness for others' thoughts and feelings, and the social negotiations that attend these concerns, can certainly affect the efficiency of group decision-making compared to solo decision-making.

In terms of strong social wayfinding then, when selecting travel partners, effective wayfinding may depend on three factors; familiarity with the terrain, an ability to distinguish between being confident and correct about your sense of direction, and social mindfulness. Better then, to travel with someone who either knows the area, isn't overconfident about their sense of direction, or who listens to your views. All three would be ideal.

Just as important as strong social wayfinding, weak social wayfinding also influences our ability to get from A to B. For lone travellers, it is more important. In weak social wayfinding one or more person (crowds, bystanders) unintentionally communicates about route choices; the so-called 'wisdom of crowds' effect (Galton, 1907).

Usually, cues are communicated unidirectionally and from further away than in strong social wayfinding scenarios. As with strong social wayfinding, weak social wayfinding may be synchronous (from people who are in the same place at the same time), or asynchronous (traces of people no longer present). An example of the former would be seeing people on a bridge or path ('Oh, that looks safe'). More enigmatically, an example of weak asynchronous social wayfinding may be litter, footprints or the dying embers of a campfire ('Other people have been here. It's probably safe', or 'Look at the size of those footprints – let's get the hell out of here'). These so-called social trails or desire lines (paths through the environment) communicate the safety or popularity of routes and spaces. Litter, noise, broken windows, graffiti, vapour trails, a lingering odour, may all influence our conclusions about whether to hang around a place.

Social wayfinding is also influenced by technology. Effective wayfinding in an unfamiliar environment often involves the use of smartphones. One study in Brisbane, Australia, compared the use of wayfinding strategies by participants using paper maps, smartphones apps or local signage. New arrivals to the city were given a two-hour pedestrian wayfinding task, such as looking for a specific location (Vaez et al., 2020). The app group were more anti-social, asking for directions less often than the other two groups. The local signage group used wayfinding strategies such as edge-following ('I presume this highway leads somewhere'), compassing ('I'll go north from here') more than the other two groups did. They also used social navigation ('I see people walking this way') more often. App-based navigating was associated with slower walking, since additional checking stops were used. Paper map users were better at memorising turns. This suggests that digital navigation changes how we interact during wayfinding (McCullough & Collins, 2018). Less sociable app navigators often ignored weak social wayfinding cues (other people), whereas signage and paper map groups heeded the wisdom of crowds. Some app users were so committed to their digital strategies as to fail to notice as they walked directly past destinations that were part of their task. For better or for worse, the use of smartphones and artificial intelligence is undoubtedly a feature of navigation and wayfinding. Although holograms and robot guides are common in tourism, these can still resemble people, true to the tradition of social wayfinding. In the context of human-robot interactions, it has been found that people prefer robot guides that resemble humans to those that are disembodied (Tussyadiah, 2020).

Whether in its strong, collaborative form or in its weak, unintentional form, the role of other people (or things that look like people) in influencing our decisions can be as co-decider, route instructor, or provider of environmental cues. All of which demonstrates the crucial role of others in guiding our travel decisions (Dalton, 2019).

AN INTERPRETIVE CRAFT: EXPERIENTIAL, EMBODIED, SENSORY WAYFINDING

So far, we have explored wayfinding as problem solving, internal map-making and social activity. But besides being intellectual and inter-personal, negotiating landscapes is also experiential, and has been studied phenomenologically through first-hand experiences of the body and senses of the traveller (Merleau-Ponty, 1963).

Wayfinding is not just about finding the shortest distance between A and B. We frequently use longer, or more enjoyable routes, perhaps to suit our sensory or physical preferences, or just for the experience. The phenomenology of wayfinding empha-sises experiential, embodied, sensory aspects of moving through landscapes. From this perspective, travel routes are immersive events, rather than necessary intervals between points ('Are we there yet?'). What happens along these routes creates meaning and memory (Cresswell, 2004). Using our bodies and senses to expe-rience journeys, routes can have as much impact on us as do the places they connect. Routes are just as important as are destina-tions (Spinney, 2006).

A phenomenological, experience-based psychology of wayfinding foregrounds feelings and experiences associated with places that are kinaesthetically sensed through our joints, muscles, tendons as we move in and across the physical world.

Haldrup & Larsen (2006: 284)

In focusing on bodies and senses, phenomenology emphasises diversity in travel experience (Symonds et al., 2017). Because bodies and senses differ so much, travel experiences are unique. Accordingly, wayfinding is less of a problem-solving activity with an agreed best solution, and more of an interpretive craft, enabling routes to be experienced differently according to various perceptions and preferences.

Wayfinding has shown to be a truly embodied activity involving physically moving the body, re-orientating the body, adjusting eyes to different light conditions.

Lueg & Bidwell (2005: 2)

Experiences of route-making are intertwined with those of others. Ingold (2011) evokes the interweaving 'meshwork' of the paths we take, which are crisscrossed and shared between us. Furthermore, each of our travel paths yield their own personal travel narratives, or 'simultaneities of stories so far' (Massey, 2005; 131). Rather than efficient, linear solutions to problems, pathways are socially shared, meandering routes ('I would normally go that way, but let's try your suggestion') that curve, bend together and borrow from each other (Ingold, 2011).

How we experience the paths we make is further influenced by our sensory engagement with landscape, which in turn differs across modes of transport. A car journey may feel more removed from the elements; less physical than a walk or journey on a bicycle (Spinney, 2006). A train journey presents the landscapes as something visual, whizzing past at speed, whilst walking in a forest enables us to hear, feel, smell and touch. Similarly, negotiating a route through a city is affected by the sensory preferences that different people have (sight, sound, touch). Tactile information can be useful, especially for travellers with visual impairments. Touch-based wayfinding is also affected by whether we travel alone. In one case study, after migrating from Spain, a new arrival to an English city learned the layout of her neighbourhood over an eighteen-month period, primarily by using her senses of sound and touch whilst walking with (being guided by, and guiding) her guide dog (Stevenson, 2017). During daily, familiarising walks, new routes were explored and navigated by the learning of sounds and tactile cues (traffic, underfoot textures, music emanating from shops), and by the shared, sensory and co-produced experience of walking in a human-dog team. Walking as a pair, human and dog developed knowledge, acquired between two bodies, about the landscape as they negotiated safe routes, always learning from the environment and from each other. This case study highlights the diverse nature of wayfinding experience, mediated through the senses, using inter-corporeal teamwork (bodies working together). This reminds us that the primacy of the visual sense is not universal.

The experience of route-making is also mediated by dynamics of power (Symonds et al., 2017). Often, we take routes which are available, advised, allowed, rather than preferred. Even within the airport confines we are steered one way or another by the powers that be. Individual agency is surrendered as bodies are ushered through walkways, past retail outlets (in the hope of a transaction), away from VIP areas or places of restricted access. This form of 'power steering' often uses sensorial cues (bright colours, warm air, aroma of coffee or perfume) to lead us astray. Beyond the airport, we can be treated as docile bodies too. In streets and shopping centres, during leisure or business travel, responsibility for wayfinding experience can be delegated to travel organisers, for instance on guided tours (Foucault & Sheridan, 1991). Travellers often submit to pre-planned, carefully controlled travel itineraries which lack opportunities to wander. Could a lack of agency be a positively liberating feature of travel? Package deals and guided tours offer comfort, knowledge and an atmosphere of reassurance that (perhaps thankfully) where we go is beyond our control. Surrendering responsibility for wayfinding may be welcomed because of added safety (Urry, 2005), the convenience of local knowledge, or

just because it makes life easier ('They organise everything for you!').
On the other hand, it undermines any sense of exploration.

Besides voluntarily handing over responsibilities for travel decisions, wayfinding can also be affected by involuntarily experienced
mediators of power. Concerns about safety or sexual harassment
inform route choices. Potential feelings of anxiety are often reduced
in a bounded, controlled environment like a cruise ship or airport,
compared with the heightened sense of anxiety we tend to experience in the less regulated city streets. Clearly, our bodies are often
subject to outside forces which compromise our wayfinding capabil-
ities. Power influences our embodied practice of wayfinding, sometimes deterring the urge to wander.

In this chapter we have learned about wayfinding as a craft, experienced through the body and senses, and as an exercise in problem-solving and internal mapmaking. We have also acknowledged the
role of other people, present or not, in directing wayfinding behaviour. Arguably the psychology of wayfinding has paid too little attention to the body over the years. Symonds et al. (2017) seek to redress
this balance by offering a more inclusive definition of wayfinding as a

Cognitive, social and corporeal process and experience of locating, following or discovering a route through and to a given space.
(2)

3

INFLUENCERS AND TRIP ADVISORS: THE SOCIAL PSYCHOLOGY OF TRAVEL

ALMOST IMPOSSIBLE TO GO IT ALONE: THE SOCIAL NATURE OF TRAVEL

It's hard to go it alone. There are almost always other people around when we travel, whether they are known to us or not. The decisions we make about where, when and how to travel are usually made with others in mind, and in the vicinity, even if we are not deliberately travelling with them. For example, have you ever selected a destination in order to stay away from the crowds? Have you ever avoided a bus, cafe or beach because it was full? Other people exert social influence on our travel plans. Journeys are made in populated spaces. Whether walking, pedalling, driving or flying, travel engages us in social situations. We travel amongst families, friends, fellow travellers, bystanders, holograms and residents of the places we pass through and visit. Social aspects of travel deserve more attention than they have received from psychologists (van Acker et al., 2010). To better understand travel behaviour, we must go beyond individual motivations, attitudes and characteristics, and view it as a social activity.

To illustrate the social nature of travel, consider the process of planning a commuter, business, or tourist trip. We might see our choice of where and how we travel as simply reflecting individual attitudes about destinations and modes of transport (*I am going there*

DOI: 10.4324/9781003215530-3

because I like it, and I am travelling this way because I enjoy it); a form of individual choice. But the connecting line between cognition (what we think), affect (what we feel) and behaviour (what we do) in relation to travel may not be a straight one. Social psychologists have historically highlighted the tenuous link between attitude, intention and behaviour (Ajzen & Fishbein, 1980). Travel may not simply reflect an individual belief or desire being put into action. Rather, these decisions are frequently swayed or compromised by other people, known to us or otherwise (*'No one else wants to go'*, *'It will be too busy'*, *'People don't usually go there'*, *'Everybody else is going, so let's go'*).

The potential disconnect between attitude and action is illustrated by the Theory of Reasoned Action (Fishbein, 1980), which considers the role played by rational decision-making in planning behaviour. It suggests that attitudes and behaviour are not always concordant, partly because of other people. Someone who perceives cycling as healthy, fun and eco-friendly may not actually get on a bike. The Theory of Reasoned Action states that a positive attitude produces intentions to do something, but that these intentions may be subsequently influenced by factors such as safety, regulation or prevailing social norms. In other words, our attitudes influence our intentions, but these can still be inhibited by social pressure (van Acker et al., 2010). Following the Theory of Reasoned Action, the Theory of Planned Behaviour (Ajzen, 1991) reinforces the view that irrespective of attitude and intention, some decisions are beyond our individual control (Ajzen, 1991). The Theory of Planned Behaviour adds an extra factor to the decision-making workflow by recognising the importance of perceived behavioural control in converting attitudes into actions. Thus, the likelihood of getting on that bike, or of visiting that beach, is additionally affected by how much we think we can carry out the desired behaviour. The Theory of Planned Behaviour proposes that travel decisions are not just down to intention. They are also influenced by how much control we think we have over our putting these good intentions into practice (based on opportunity, time, social norms and so forth).

According to another influential social psychological theory, inconsistencies between attitudes and action, or between two simultaneously held attitudes ('*I love flying but I realise that it is bad for the environment*') can manifest themselves as a sense of discomfort, known as cognitive dissonance (Festinger, 1957). This unease can then influence how likely it is that attitudes translate into action. Harbouring two incompatible attitudes, or an attitude ('*I disagree with frequent flying*') that is inconsistent with a behaviour ('*I flew here*'), is uncomfortable for us and we are motivated to reduce this feeling. To do so, we either change one of those attitudes (rationalising), or we alter an attitude in line with behaviour we have already carried out ('*Well that flight would have taken off anyway, with or without me on it, and anyway lots of people fly every day*'). Feelings of discomfort from cognitive dissonance are commonplace when travelling. For example, when reflecting on a chosen travel mode or destination, we sometimes experience post-decision dissonance, perhaps when opting for a less environmentally friendly journey which jars with our green credentials. Reducing this kind of dissonance might, as one study found, involve using positive online reviews to support our choice ('*Lots of other people take internal flights, so I think I did the right thing after all*'). It is also common to seek out more favourable reviews online to support our decisions, whilst at the same time overlooking less favourable ones, in order to reduce feelings of dissonance (Tanford & Montgomery, 2015). In situations like these, we look for what others are doing to help us justify sometimes uncomfortable choices.

These aforementioned theories (Reasoned Action, Planned Behaviour, Cognitive Dissonance) acknowledge the potential rift between reason, intention and action. Several factors, like social norms and circumstance, explain why attitudes and actions do not always go hand in hand. Some of these factors relate closely to travel habits which are hard to break, and which are reinforced by what everyone else is doing (van Acker et al., 2010). Indeed, some of our habitual travel decisions seem to positively defy logic and rational decision making. For example, we may decide against taking the most direct, stress-free, or environmentally friendly routes, or be reluctant to adapt to different modes of travel (walking to work, travelling by train, car sharing) merely out of entrenched habit ('*My family have always travelled this way'*). Whilst an initial visit to a place may be based on rational decision making, once a travel routine becomes ingrained, rational, attitude-based decision making takes a back seat, according to the Theory of Repeated Behaviour (Ronis et al., 1989). Changing a routine, even in line with a logical, stated belief, can be challenging (Gärling & Axhausen, 2003). All the theories mentioned so far suggest that travel habits can be ingrained or affected because of factors beyond individual free will, cognitions or intentions. As travellers we are at the mercy of established routines, social norms and other circumstances which prevent us converting our intentions into actions. The social context of travel can help us see how other people influence the tenuous link between attitudes and actions.

GROUP TRAVEL, HABITS AND HABITUS

The art of planning a journey requires us to take account of everyday social realities (De Certeau, 1984) such as likely social encounters (wanted or unwanted), social identity (*'Will I fit in? Do I really belong to this group?'*), social influence (what everyone else is doing). Whilst we may be able to influence some of these factors, the messiness of social life means that many are beyond our control. Where and how we travel depends on how much we identify with or feel comfortable in certain social situations. A perceived lack of social competence, skill or habitus (Bourdieu, 1984) that might enable us to thrive in a social situation like a cruise, a hen party, or a retreat, may lead us to decline those travel opportunities. Choices about the milieus we think we belong to (for example, due to spending capacity, or perceived social competence) impinge on both daily and occasional travel (Guell et al., 2012). Commuting, holidaying, migrating, driving, flying, walking and cycling are all social practices that attract people from differing but overlapping social groups, with certain demographics, social skills and identities. A decision, for example, about whether to cycle to work may be made partly due to cost or safety but may also be influenced by feelings of belongingness to a group, reflecting how we define ourselves in terms of our social identity (Aldred, 2010).

Similarly, a decision to go on a cruise or to travel by coach to a football game, may partly be influenced by whether we see ourselves as fitting in with social groups known as 'cruisers' or 'football fans', as much as by the practicalities of the decision. This said, identification with a particular travel group is not fixed (Guell et al., 2012). We can change our allegiance as material and social conditions change.

From a social psychological perspective, all travel, to some extent, is group travel. Many travel groupings are distinguished because of their mode of travel and the skills, attitudes and habits that are part and parcel of feeling like, say, a biker, rambler, or frequent flyer. What emerges here is that there are several varieties of travel groupings, each with their own norms and social identities.

THE VISITORS AND THE VISITED: TRAVELLER TYPOLOGIES

Whilst there are many types of travellers, including migrants, commuters, adventurers and day-trippers, there has been little attempt in the psychological literature to construct a comprehensive typology in terms of motivations or characteristics. However, leisure travellers have been grouped, sorted and categorised, both anecdotally and in print. For example, backpackers, sojourners and explorers frequently seek to distance themselves (both literally and metaphorically) from tourists and holidaymakers. In his novel about clashing cultures of North America and North Africa, The Sheltering Sky, Paul Bowles (1949) famously distinguished tourists, who enjoy visiting diverse locations for short periods, from travellers, who seem equally comfortable for long periods in transit as they do in their own homes. Leisure travellers (whether tourists or travellers) are a heterogeneous group (Fan, 2017), with varying motivations and characteristics. Traveller types are regularly identified by people-spotters in airports and resorts, as they were by Cohen (1984) in an article which distinguishes 'mass tourists' from 'explorers and drifters'. Mass tourists, wrote Cohen, do their travelling from behind the protective wall of travel industry representatives who do most of the organising and booking for them. Interactions with hosts are carefully choreographed, centred around designated sites and destinations. Meanwhile, 'explorers and drifters' travel relatively unprotected and are likely to have direct contact with culturally diverse people as they wander away from the beaten track.

A further five-fold traveller typology was identified by Fan (2017), who distinguished between *dependents, conservatives, criticizers, explorers* and *belonging-seekers*, primarily in relation to differing forms of contact with inhabitants of host communities (locals). Whilst based on a study of visitors to mainland China, this typology can be used to understand the motivations of leisure travellers more generally. The first group, *dependents*, typically travel in established groups (friends, relatives, parties) as part of a package tour, on short-term visits, and willfully avoid interactions with hosts. Dependents show little interest in mixing with locals, despite being keen to visit their locale. The second group, *conservatives* have more host contact, though mainly for purposes of gaining information or guidance. Before the advent of smartphones or social media this might have involved asking for directions or travel recommendations. More recently, conservatives' communications with hosts might typically involve speaking with indigenous tourist representatives, hotel staff, tour guides or taxi drivers. This constitutes relatively shallow contact, such as seeking local knowledge, although it would also likely contribute to a positive retrospective, if generalising, impression of a place ('*the people were so nice, so helpful*'). Thirdly, *criticizers*, tend to be more self-directed and experienced travellers. They are likely to interact with hosts a little more. They regularly have service-oriented conversations and casually converse with hosts, whilst at the same time remaining relatively detached from local communities. Despite having more knowledge of a host culture, criticizers view hosts through their own cultural lens, and often make judgments based on prior ('*I know best*'), established attitudes. A fourth group, *explorers*, are also experienced travellers, though are open to greater social contact with hosts, going out of their way to engage in social interaction with locals. They are eager to find out about them through casual conversation, often in the local language. Explorers determinedly stray into non-tourist sites and seek out locations that are off the well-worn tourist trail. Host contact meaningfully impacts attitudes and perceptions of explorers, often changing preconceived ideas about a group or place. Of the five groups, the fifth, *belonging seekers*, are certainly more travellers than tourists. They engage with locals at a relatively deep level, sharing experiences, participating in daily life and establishing non-utilitarian friendships. Where possible and if invited, they visit host homes and share authentic indigenous cultural experiences, and are most likely to report enhanced, positive attitudes of a place and its residents. Belonging seekers are the most likely to extend their visits, seek employment or voluntary work in host communities, learn the language and remain culturally attached.

Though necessarily rather general and mainly applicable to the field of leisure travel, these tourist typologies help us understand varieties of traveller motivations in terms of attitudes towards host communities. They can also be seen as fluid, rather than fixed, typologies. For example, whilst a visitor may begin as a conservative, the passage of time and cultivation of interest may see them flourish into a belonging-seeker. Traveller types differ in relation to openness and desire to explore visited communities. However, despite these differing groups, perhaps the two social groups who have attracted the most attention from social psychologists are not the different varieties of travellers, but the broader groups of travellers and hosts.

CAN TOURISM HELP US TO GET ALONG?

Whilst rarely a reason for travel, encounters between locals and travellers are an inevitable consequence of tourism. Traveller-host encounters often influence pre-existing attitudes about people from other cultures, since intergroup contact mediates our understanding of outgroups. Meetings between locals and travellers inform stereotypes and may even improve intergroup relations (Kirillova et al., 2015). Travel and intercultural encounter have the capacity to reduce anxiety, mediate distrust and enhance empathy between groups (Dovidio et al., 2002). Tourism has even been explicitly identified as a positive factor for promoting peace between different cultures (Gursoy & Nunkoo, 2019).

According to the contact hypothesis (Allport, 1979) encounters between people from different cultures, facilitated by travel, can enhance intercultural perceptions. The theory proposes that intergroup contact reduces prejudice and improves relations under certain conditions. For example, where there is equal status between representatives of groups, prejudice reduction is likely. Other fertile conditions for improved relations are agreed cultural values (about dress codes, diet or noise level tolerance) and opportunities for informal personal interaction. Under such circumstances, travellers to new destinations can often form lasting friendships and improve their cultural understanding (Pratt & Liu, 2015). Without such favourable conditions, prejudice, discrimination and hostility can be associated with intercultural contact (Sherif, 1966). Problematically, tourism often involves contact between people in unequal status situations. Relatively privileged travellers mix with hosts who work in hotels, restaurants, or as travel guides, who have lower levels of income than their visitors. Thus, interaction between tourists and local people is often restricted to brief, shallow, unequal interactions (Dilek, 2016), potentially undermining opportunities for meaningful contact or reduced prejudice.

Contact hypothesis helps us understand the likelihood of positive outcomes between tourists and hosts and the dangers of encounters between groups with differing economic circumstances or cultural norms (Çelik, 2019a). As tourists and locals mingle, exchanging goods or information (Yilmaz & Taşçı, 2015), the contact hypothesis would predict prejudice reduction in the absence of status differences, historical (colonial) conflicts between groups, or differing norms (Pernecky, 2015). Opportunities for tourism to improve intercultural relations depend on other factors too, like the quality of the contact, the state of pre-existing relationships between cultural groups and how enjoyable the travel experience is overall (Tomljenovic, 2010). It seems that the optimum conditions for a positive intercultural encounter on holiday would be a positive travel experience, where hosts and visitors share values and status, and are already positively disposed to one another.

In one reported case, following a German group tour to Antalya (Turkey), intergroup prejudices reportedly worsened (Sirakaya-Turk et al., 2014). Antagonistic attitudes were aggravated by a general dissatisfaction with the overall holiday experience, with the tour guide, even with the shopping facilities. Elsewhere, and more encouragingly, a visit to Russia by tourists from the U.S. coincided with a small, improved attitude towards Russian people, despite a simultaneous deterioration in attitudes towards the Russian government (Çelik, 2019a). In another 'before and after' style study, 33 Israelis visiting Egypt and 29 Egyptians visiting Israel were interviewed, with a quarter of Israelis and most of the Egyptians changing their attitudes positively (Maoz, 2010) after the travel experience. Most research linking the contact hypothesis with tourist-host interactions associates positive attitude change with travel, with some caveats relating to factors such as equal status and meaningful contact (Tomljenovic, 2010). It has therefore been suggested that tourist destinations urge visitors to stay longer, visit events organised by locals and learn more about local cultures (Çelik, 2019a).

Duration of intercultural contact can also influence attitudes towards other cultural groups. Like many other forms of human relations, tourist-host contact can progress through stages over time, not all of them harmonious. Often a honeymoon period descends into intolerance or fatigue. In popular destinations, as tourist numbers increase or as the tourist season wears on, the patience of hosts can wear thin (Brida et al , 2010). Initial euphoria at the economic benefits of attracting visitors can give way to apathy, annoyance and antagonism (Boğan & Sarıışık, 2016). Declining levels of tolerance in tourist host interactions can see them go from *embracement* (locals accept tourists) to *tolerance* (locals indecisive or ambivalent), to *adjustment* (locals try and prevent tourists from visiting), then *withdrawal* (locals want to leave and/or express hostility) (Ap & Crompton, 1993). It appears that many people who live in popular tourist spots welcome visitors up to a point, at least initially.

Host-visitor contact can also influence intercultural attitudes beyond the context of tourism. For example, there is evidence of travel affecting attitudes following immigration (Moufakkir, 2013). When members of a relatively unknown outgroup take up long term residence in a community, intercultural attitudes can change. Tension may arise between majority culture hosts and visiting minorities, such as immigrants. Here too, stages of acceptance often unfold. For example, in the case of Moroccan immigrants in the Netherlands, initial accept-ance reportedly gave way to fatigue and animosity (Moufakkir, 2013), with an interesting knock-on effect too. Negative attitudes towards the visiting outgroup influenced subsequent attitudes of travellers who then visited North Africa. Interviews with participants from the Neth-erlands suggested that first contacts with intercultural outgroup visi-tors at home had an influence on future attitudes towards hosts during travel. According to this dynamic, immigration and tourism interact with each other in relation to attitude change. Hence, Dutch peoples' perceptions about Moroccan residents in the Netherlands affected their appetite for visiting Morocco. It appears that in a globalised world, first impressions of particular cultural groups often take place not at the tourist destination, but before travel, following domestic encounters. First impressions of a tourist destination, it seems, often begin in your own city, shop or restaurant.

Travel, whether it be tourism or immigration, is a key site of inter-cultural encounter. Meaningful, equal status contact between cultural groups with similar values appears to be a positive force for inter-cultural relations. Problematically, tourism and immigration cannot always provide these forms of contact.

TRIP ADVISING: SOCIAL INFLUENCE AND TRAVEL CHOICE

Social influence, a signature topic of social psychology, is concerned with how behaviour changes in the light of others' actions. Several varieties of social influence have been identified (Kelman, 1958). For example, the term *compliance* is used to describe a situation where behaviours of others are adopted, yet private, perhaps dissenting, opinions remain unaffected (*'You can change the way I act, but not how I think'*). Outwardly we follow suit, inwardly we retain our individuality. A second term, *identification*, refers to taking on others' views or behav-iours in order to maintain a relationship with them, keep them on our side, or be liked (*'If I agree with them, perhaps I will be accepted as part of their* group'). Thirdly, *internalisation* is when the influence of others is enough to produce internal, attitudinal, as well as behavioural, change ('*I agree with him and will act accordingly*'). When making travel choices we are often guided by what others say or do. Word of mouth, guidebooks, online reviews, greatly affect our travel plans. We might see this as an example of internalisation, wherein our internal views, intentions and external actions are all swayed by friends, family, travel experts or online influencers. Alternatively, if we take a trip with another person in order to please them, whilst internally remaining ambivalent about it this might be described as identification.

Whilst it is common for online trip-advising strangers to influence our travel decisions, the level of expertise of these influencers is not always especially high. We seem not to rely on online influencers being travel experts when seeking their opinions. Rather, qualities such as the recency of a post, or how factually accurate it seems to be, are more desirable qualities of a review (Vermeulen & Seegers, 2009; Ayeh et al., 2013). Expert or otherwise, trip advice about choosing a particular hotel, travelling sustainably or opting for a walking route, greatly influence purchasing decisions (Hsu & Huang, 2012; von Bergner & Lohmann, 2013). User-generated reviews are arguably the most important promotional tools in travel marketing (Shu-Chuan & Kim, 2018). Most travellers with access to social media spend over two hours surfing for information about a trip (Nielsen, 2015), looking for guidance from strangers who have already experienced what they are about to (Bilgihan et al., 2016).

To paraphrase Facebook CEO Mark Zuckerberg, nothing influences people more than a recommendation from a trusted friend. These days, trusted friends typically belong to online influencer communities. Online word of mouth has overtaken old school alternatives (asking neighbours and friends) as the go-to source of travel guidance. The online family is now the prime user-generated influencer for tourists and travellers. Over three-quarters of travellers consult online customer reviews when booking hotels (Shu-Chuan & Kim, 2018.), revealing a positive correlation between purchase intentions and positive reviews (Tanford & Montgomery, 2015). Where income allows, many customers will pay more for hotels that have better reviews (Fillieri & McLeay, 2014).

In a study investigating socially influenced travel purchases, predictably, participants were significantly less likely to choose a resort with just a minority of favourable reviews. More surprisingly, having a majority of favourable reviews was no more appealing than having no reviews at all. In other words, a small minority of negative reviews severely damaged a resort's appeal (Tanford & Montgomery, 2015). Endorsing this 'one bad apple' effect, in a famous social psychological laboratory experiment, Solomon Asch (1956) demonstrated that participants' decision-making was far more heavily influenced by others where those other opinions were unanimously held. As in Tanford's research into online trip advice, one dissenting voice was shown to have a considerable effect in undermining the majority view. Where trip advice is concerned, one 1-star review can undo all the work of a long list of glowing 5-star tributes.

As well as influencing consumer travel decisions, social influence can affect the behaviour of the reviewers themselves; a case of influencers influencing influencers. One study found the linguistic style of online travel reviews rubbed off on other reviewers. Comparing the stock phrases, linguistic tics and adjectives used in positive (5-star) restaurant reviews with those used by punters giving 4 stars or less, it was found each group used very similar vocabulary (Shu-Chuan & Kim, 2018). Five-star rating or not, similar uses of vocabulary suggest a social influence effect among reviewers. This suggests that reviewers read other reviews to help them compose their own, suggesting that social influence affects the reviewing style of posters as well as the purchasing patterns of consumers (Oliveira et al., 2020).

Why do some of us feel the need to offer travel tips to people we will never meet? One attraction of posting reviews may be the resulting feeling of belongingness to, or togetherness with, our fellows in the imagined community of travellers. Writing travel advice arguably satisfies a need to be helpful, or to be accepted by peers (Shu-Chuan & Kim, 2018). This aligns with the aforementioned variety of social influence known as identification (Kelman, 1958). It has also been suggested that sharing travel recommendations is motivated by altruism (Munar & Jacobsen, 2014), or by a desire for increased self-esteem (Oliveira et al., 2020). Does this reveal a need to identify with other online users by sharing travel blunders and discoveries? Posting advice to help others, or to feel acceptance, suggests that we glean a form of attachment motivation from participating in online travel communities. We satisfy a desire to share, help and maintain relationships with others.

Besides altruism and identification, various other rewards have been put forward as motivations for trip advising, ranging from enjoyment, a desire to exert power over large companies, venting negative affect (letting off steam), raising self-esteem or wanting to become an influencer (Yoo & Gretzel, 2008). Trip advisors vary markedly in tone and motive. They have been variously labelled as *altruists* (predisposed to help), *careerists* (keen to spark discussion and become influencers), *hipsters* (seeking identification or connectedness), *boomerangs* (comment and like seekers), and *connectors* (keen to share experiences) (Brett, 2011). Yet not every traveller writes reviews. A large, silent majority of so-called *lurkers* use travel reviews without exerting their own influence (Munar & Jacobsen, 2014). Perhaps they abstain from posting because of concerns over security (Osatuyi, 2015), or because of personality traits such as low self-esteem (Preece et al., 2004). Whatever the reason, we should keep in mind that despite the undoubted social influence of online reviews, most content is produced by a vocal minority of travellers (Sun et al., 2014).

Social influence theory helps us to understand various aspects of travel behaviour, including purchasing patterns and the urge to share travel advice. By absorbing the experiences of others, learning from their howlers and travel highs, we change our behaviours, attitudes and purchasing habits, arguably through a process of internalisation (Oliveira et al., 2020), adapting how we think and how we act. Additionally, we may share travel content, offering advice which helps us feel helpful, influential or socially accepted (Sedera et al., 2017). Perhaps through identifying with others (Kelman, 1974), travel influencers and casual posters can develop a sense of belongingness to a community of strangers, a process which might also afford a sense of social identity and self-esteem (Zhou, 2011). We should also make clear that, aside from these apparent psychological rewards of online travel advising, on a practical level, sharing experiences is both enjoyable and helpful to those of us who are keen to avoid negative travel experiences.

4

TRAVEL FEVER: A WORRYING WORLD OF FEAR, PHOBIA AND ANXIETY

FEAR, ANXIETY, PHOBIA AND WORRY

Though ideally pleasurable, travel can make us feel uneasy. It is fraught with potentially justifiable fears (of being hijacked, getting lost, losing belongings), anxieties (about being away from home), worries (about being late, missing connections) and phobias (of crowds, aeroplanes, open spaces, confined spaces). But how are these distinct, and why are so many of them associated with travel? In this chapter we will try to answer some of these questions, using psychological research to enlighten us.

Fear has biochemical and emotional components (Fennell, 2017). The former provokes sweating, increased heart rate and high adrenaline levels, making us extremely alert. The emotional components of fear can be experienced positively (pleasure, excitement) or negatively (avoidance, distress). For those people who are thrill-seekers, or who happen to be in a carefree mood, fear is more likely to be experienced as a pleasurable emotion. For those with a cautious disposition or mood, fear will be experienced negatively. Whilst biochemical fear may be the same for all of us, the emotional response may be good or bad, depending on personality or mood. In either case, fear is useful for signalling danger or threat. It alerts us to take adaptive,

DOI: 10.4324/9781003215530-4

precautionary measures; the so-called fight or flight response. In the context of travel, a valuable fear response might lead us to avoid or vacate spaces that are perceived as threatening.

Fear is typically directed towards a specific threat, like a suspicious-looking fellow traveller, an unattended package or a stray dog. It focuses on known, identifiable, external dangers (Steimer, 2002). Contrastingly, anxiety is a generalized response to a non-specific threat, experienced as an ill-defined internal conflict or uneasiness. Fear's object is external, known and in our sights. Anxiety's origin is uncertain. It is often accompanied by a lack of control or feelings of uncertainty, making coping difficult. We sometimes feel anxious about leaving our familiar surroundings, though without any identifiable focus reason why.

When fears are experienced more intensely, even requiring treatment, we deem them to be phobias. Phobias impair normal functioning, provoke consistent avoidance behaviour and are regarded as irrational. Around 10% of people experience a phobia during their lifetime, although rates of diagnosis range from 3% in some cultures to 15% in others (Eaton et al., 2018). Your chance of being diagnosed with a phobia rises in higher income countries, where incidentally international travel is also more affordable and common. These differences are likely due to the quality and availability of differing assessment and diagnostic instruments across cultures (Eaton et al., 2018). Both fear reactions and phobic diagnosis are culturally relative, and so are triggered differently in different places. For example, *Taijin Kyofusho*, a form of social phobia, is reportedly unique to Japanese and Korean cultures (Essau et al., 2013). Other countries demonstrate a common fear of international terrorism, refugees, or of people from specific countries with whom they share borders. According to one report, Poles can be disproportionately fearful of people from Russia (Borger et al., 2015). Some of the fears mentioned here (e.g. social phobia, xenophobia) are related to travel and tourism. Furthermore, the age group most likely to report a phobia is mid-life to old age; again, those most likely to be able to afford to travel, for leisure at least. Several common phobic objects, such as planes, open spaces, strangers, are also synonymous with travel.

Besides fear, phobia and anxiety, travel can also be accompanied by more moderate feelings of worry. Like fear, worry is less generalised and visceral than anxiety (Winch, 2014). We may worry specifically about getting to the airport on time, whilst having a more generalised anxiety about travel. Looking on the bright side, worry can be quite constructive. It is more likely to trigger problem-solving than, say, anxiety, which befuddles us and makes solutions less likely. Although the terms fear and worry can be used interchangeably, fear is usually prompted by a specific danger (heights, loud noises or air travel). Worry is a milder feeling that something bad might happen (missing an aeroplane, getting lost).

Evidently there is plenty to concern us about travel. A journey may be hampered by generalised anxiety, specific fears, debilitating phobias, or a milder worry. Fear and worry are quite distressing. Anxiety is more powerful, disruptive and problematic. A phobia (for example, of flying) is likely to effect a change of itinerary. Fear and worry can be helpful and facilitate strategies to deal with their sources. They are part of normal functioning. Phobias and anxiety are often pathological and may require treatment.

TRAVEL FEVER: ORIGINS, VARIETIES AND SOURCES

Fear-like, physiological or emotional responses to travel have been recognised as a nervous condition since the 19th century, when leisure travel became an option for privileged European elites (Zencker et al., 2021). Diagnostic labels like travel fever denoted a form of imbalanced restlessness or overstimulation which combined

> simultaneous feelings of anticipation or longing for the unknown and fear of temporarily abandoning safe home environments.
> (Zencker et al., 2021: 2)

Travel fever pulls us in two directions. It combines nervous anticipation of entering the unknown with uncertainty about what is being left behind. Whether travelling short or long haul, and for whatever purpose, there are plenty of potential sources of travel fever, which may manifest themselves as fear, anxiety, phobia or worry. Every stage of a journey (planning, departing, being somewhere new, returning, even reminiscing) can elicit fear or anxiety (Fennell, 2017). At various points along a journey, specific sources of travel fear might include unfamiliar spaces or food, excessive speed, even injections (often a requirement of international travel). One study found nearly 40% of travellers feared injections (Noble et al., 2013).

Arrival in unfamiliar destinations can usher in a whole world of worry, fear or anxiety. Unfamiliar food is a common source of fear. Food tourists in Asia reported concern over unidentifiable meats, with culturally specific foods such as reptile or dog being especially associated with fear responses in visitors from countries where these are absent from the menu (Cohen & Avieli, 2004). Even tourist attractions, perhaps the very reason for travelling in the first place, can induce fear. For adventure tourists, maybe such risks are what make attractions attractive in the first place (Stone & Sharpley, 2008). The physical danger of climbing a mountain, swimming with dolphins or wild camping, may be part of the appeal. Beyond adventure travel, participating in mundane activities in unfamiliar surroundings has its dangers too; large crowds, heights, heavy traffic, the risk of getting lost, overzealous police or enforced contact with people from unfamiliar cultural groups. U.S. travellers visiting non-westernised countries have reported fear reactions linked to encounters with unfamiliar life habits and standards of cleanliness (Kingsbury et al., 2012). Encountering cultural difference can manifest itself as culture shock, defined as

> a series of related psychological reactions developing over time
> with continued exposure to an alien culture.
> (Cort & King, 1979: 212)

Fear of difference is especially prevalent where travellers encounter unfamiliar artefacts, signs or symbols ('*What does this street sign say?*'), perhaps leading to withdrawal, hostility towards locals or generalised anxiety. Susceptibility to culture-shock is not universal however and depends on factors such as prior travel experience (McKercher & Lui, 2013). Those who are unaccustomed to encountering diverse cultures are most likely to be unsettled by new experiences and to yearn for familiarity. It has also been found that people who are generally intolerant of ambiguity in their everyday lives (lovers of order and tidiness) are particularly susceptible to culture-shock anxiety (Cort & King, 1979). Intolerance of unpredictability makes independent travel a particularly unsettling experience.

In extreme cases, travel fear gets out of control. Travel phobia, involving excessive or unreasonable fear and avoidance behaviours, can affect passengers on public transport, motorists, motorcyclists, cyclists or pedestrians (de Jongh et al., 2011). Whatever the mode of transport, travel phobia often attaches itself to experiences which are integral to encountering new places. When visiting somewhere new (to us) we often find ourselves in unfamiliar open spaces (and may feel agoraphobic), small spaces (claustrophobic), crowded spaces (demophobic), on busy roads (hodophobic), flights (aviophobic), or at risk of infection (nosophobic). COVID-19 spurned labels used to describe persistent, disruptive fear of travel during a pandemic, such as coronaphobia, or the more generalised coronavirus anxiety (Asmundson & Taylor, 2020). The wide range of available travel-related phobias reflects the diversity of experiences that travel offers. We have plenty of phobic objects to choose from, although in truth they rather choose us; other people, animals, natural phenomena (storms, heights, water), human-made phenomena (vehicles, flying, confined spaces), illness and physical injury (Torgersen et al., 2000). That many of these phobic objects present perceptible risks is undeniable, and so it is debatable as to whether these are irrational phobias or justifiable fears. For most travellers, whilst they would constitute legitimate sources of fear to be acknowledged and guarded against, they would not prevent travel altogether (Fennell, 2017).

Besides the aforementioned specific sources of travel fear, a more generalised anxiety associated with travel and tourism has been identified, by the American Psychiatric Association, as a psychological condition with cognitive, behavioural, emotional and physiological dimensions (APA, 2013). Travel anxiety ('I have a bad feeling about this journey'), like specific fears, can be triggered at various points on a journey, leading to somatic (physiological) and cognitive symptoms (distressing thoughts). Anxiety provoking pinch points include trip preparation, financial uncertainty, transport dangers, destination and activity unknowns, accommodation, physical safety (Minnaert, 2014). Even before setting off, anticipatory anxiety (persistent distress about future travel) can produce somatic (insomnia, dizziness) or cognitive symptoms (distress, worry). These may prevent travel altogether and lead to panic attacks or depression (Lee, 2020).

Travel fears and anxieties can lead to interruptions or cancellations to our journeys. This is partly because they are often experienced physically, as well as psychologically.

THE EMBODIMENT OF FEAR AND ANXIETY

Fear responses to leaving home and entering the unknown can be visceral and embodied. We feel travel fever, rather than just being cognizant of it. Travel fear and anxiety are responses to physical dangers encountered in transit for bodies which, especially when in unfamiliar territory, are always at risk (Symonds, 2017). Indeed, because we are on high alert during travel, we often design or modify our routes on a safety-first basis, even if this sometimes means travelling a little further ('I will avoid that short-cut, it may be dangerous'). The positive correlation between the perception of travel risk and feelings of anxiety is well-known (Reisinger & Manondo, 2005). Embodied, anxious responses to perceived emotional, social and psychological risks all combine to form concerns about physical safety (Schiffman et al., 2012). If, for example, we are lost in an unfamiliar city, our feelings of frustration, helplessness and anger are physically, as well as cognitively, felt (Burkitt, 2014). The body is central to travel fear, and the further from home we transport it, the more fear or anxiety it is likely to experience. The further we are from home comforts and the more we surround ourselves with perceived difference, the more fearful many of us become (Sousa & Bradley, 2006). There are plenty of exceptions to this rule of course, but generally, cultural distance correlates with "psychic distance", and a perceived potential for culture-based misinterpretations and misunderstandings, again heightening risk perceptions and the experience of embodied fear and unease.

Travel during a major international health scare exemplifies how anxiety is experienced as an embodied threat. During the Ebola epidemic in West Africa in 2014, fear of touring in the region coincided with a 50% decrease in visits (even to West African countries unaffected by Ebola), up to three years after the emergency (World Travel & Tourism Council, 2018). In Gambia, despite a prolonged period without reported Ebola cases, incoming tourism halved over a two-year period (Novelli et al., 2018). Global health scares leave lasting effects on the public consciousness. International travellers respond to world events, are guided by published statistics and make difficult decisions about the safety of travel. An element of travel fear under these circumstances is understandable and rational, considering the role played by tourism in epidemic wave transmission (Widmar et al., 2017). Respiratory illnesses such as SARS (severe acute respiratory syndrome) and MERS (Middle East respiratory syndrome) both spread along crowded tourism routes (Hong Kong and Jeddah) during 2002 and 2012 respectively (Al Tawfiq et al., 2014). COVID-19, which first appeared in Wuhan, China, before spreading worldwide, inevitably stoked travel fear (Novelli et al., 2018). Aside from the threat of infection, travel restrictions, quarantine and isolation measures (used to control infection) all fuel fear amongst the public (Eichelberger, 2007). Fears are magnified and accelerated as social media enables us to observe others' reactions and experiences (Dalrymple et al., 2016). Tourists facing high risks, with restricted medical care during a pandemic outbreak, may develop a sense of helplessness and long-term anxiety towards travelling. Justifiable fears of travel following global health emergencies illustrate the physical roots of our psychological travel concerns.

Whilst it is difficult to accurately assess COVID-19's effect on perceived travel risk, there have been attempts to engage with this problem psychometrically. In constructing a *Pandemic Anxiety Travel Scale* (PATS), Zencker et al. (2021) set out to measure pandemic related travel anxiety. PATS seeks to measure anticipatory travel anxiety using items such as '*I am afraid to risk my life when I travel because of COVID-19*', '*When watching news about COVID-19 I become nervous or anxious about travel*', and '*I do not feel safe to travel due to COVID-19*'. Focusing on cognitive-based travel-related decision-making, PATS assesses the likelihood of reduced travel intention at a time when people are perhaps justifiably more likely to fear crowds (Zenker & Kock, 2020), unknown situations or groups who are perceived as being culturally different (Faulkner et al., 2004). In the same vein, it has been found that higher scores on xenophobia predict a lower intention to travel and a desire to avoid the unknown (Kock et al., 2019). The likelihood is that global pandemics heighten both specific travel fears, as well as more generalised anxieties about being in unfamiliar places.

Whilst scales such as PATS can help to identify changes in travel decisions based on heightened risk perception, we should remember that travel decisions are seldom based on rationally weighing up statistical probabilities alone, or physical feelings of wellness. They can also be influenced by anecdotal evidence, social media and speculation. Hence, our decisions about whether to go or stay are less than informed at times (Wang & Ackerman, 2019). As we are about to explore, travel decisions can be influenced by factors ranging from emotional responses, childhood traumas or unconscious desires.

AN UNCONSCIOUS FEAR OF FLYING

> For all but two years between 1975 and 2010, the number of fatal accidents in large aircraft could be counted on the fingers of one hand.
>
> Savage (2013: 18)

Statistically speaking, fear of flying is unfounded. Its existence illustrates a tendency to miscalculate when planning some journeys. Planes trump cars, trains, buses, ferries and motorcycles in the safety stakes. Fatal air accident risk fell by around 90% from 0.8 per million departures in the mid 1970s to less than 0.1 in 2013 (Savage, 2013). Yet these figures are insufficiently reassuring to prevent some of us from harbouring an unconscious, irrational fear of flying (aviophobia). The most acknowledged fears associated with flying relate to taking off and landing (Page, 2004). From a psychodynamic perspective, aviophobia may be down to a perfect storm of leaving the security of home (and land), entering the unknown, very quickly, at 35,000 feet, and doing all this whilst being surrounded by strangers (Kahr, 2004). This cocktail of perceived risk and uprootedness can manifest itself as a form of separation anxiety. Like many infants, some adults grow anxious when leaving behind the safety, warmth and familiarity of home. Hence, in-flight traveller separation anxiety is likely to be felt more acutely in individuals who experienced infantile separation. The adult flying experience may revive previous experiences of separation and loss, and an unconscious fear of falling (Kahr, 2004).

Traveller separation anxiety was the subject of a departure lounge-based field experiment in which the attachment behaviours of separating couples were observed (Fraley & Shaver, 2000). Couples who were separating and saying goodbye displayed more obvious attachment behaviours (clinging, holding, staying close) than those who were not. Furthermore, those who had previously reported (on a questionnaire) more anxious attachment styles showed greater distress at the prospect of separation from their partners than did those who had reported more secure attachment styles. This reinforces the parallels between separation anxieties felt during what may already be perceived as the perilous practice of flying, and the anxieties felt by some individuals during previously experienced infantile separation.

Beyond the departure lounge, having left dry land (and perhaps our significant others) behind, further parallels between infantile separation anxiety and flight anxiety emerge. Once seatbelts have been fastened the duty of care for passenger security devolves to a hopefully reassuring team of smiling, uniformed carers. Psychotherapist Brett Kahr (2004) highlights the surrogate parenting roles of onboard cabin crews. At high altitude we are passive recipients of care and attention administered by a fleet of skilled (mainly female) flight attendants, who feed and protect us and grant us occasional permission to go to the bathroom. As our role models they enact the ritual of the safety demonstration, showing us how to behave if we get into deep water. Behind the scenes, the (predominantly male) pilots, for the purposes of this analogy, play the role of absent fathers, working tirelessly to get us to where we want to go. The onboard scenario is an uncanny reconstruction of a domestic reality which is common in many (though not all) households.

Kahr's playful analogy suggests that modern passenger aircraft share many interpersonal dynamics of infantile experience, complete with an onboard parenting crew controlling safety, mealtimes, free movement and access to sanitation. And they do all this at 35,000 feet. Small wonder that this scenario elicits regressive behaviour at times; air rage, irrational fear, selfishness, oral gratification (heavy drinking). We might see air travel as a site of experience which combines reasonable fears of albeit unlikely events (crashing, terrorism) with the reignition of primitive, infantile fears (separation, falling), all taking place in a situation where unknown adults are responsible for our wellbeing. In this high-altitude capsule we entrust the cabin crew and pilot with our safety. They are our best hope of overcoming any fears that we might have.

FACING THE FEVER: MANAGING TRAVEL FEAR

An obvious coping strategy for reducing travel fear, short of not travelling, is to avoid or minimise risk. Conservative travel strategies include sticking to known, internationally branded hotels, hiring native-language guides, eating familiar food or participating in group tours (McKercher & Lui, 2013). Many of these are the bread and butter of the package tourism industry, which is founded on providing travel experiences for the risk averse. To more adventurous travellers, they take the fun out of the journey.

Conservative travel creates safe bubbles which allow us to experience new places and cultures without fully immersing ourselves in unfamiliar places. A coach trip through a busy city, a guided tour through an open-air market, a heavily supervised safari, are all viable low-risk travel tactics. Cruises are another example of supervised global exploration. Compare, for example, the risks faced on board a passenger cruise ship with those at large in the streets of an unsupervised port. The former is a safe, mobile haven, with novel, regulated experiences in exotic locations. In the port meanwhile, we can encounter otherness and experience emotions associated with entering the unknown. Traveller enclaves like cruise ships, luxury coaches, international hotels, theme parks and backpacker hostels facilitate travel without the risk of letting go of familiar comforts (Wilson & Richards, 2008). Travel bubbles are a shield against culture-shock anxiety. They can be used throughout a trip, for those who prefer to minimise risk altogether. Alternatively, they are handy safe bases for those who can tolerate intermittent immersion in novel environments.

Conservative travel bubbles offer a risk management strategy for fear reduction which illustrates so-called protection motivation theory (Zheng et al., 2021). This theory highlights a common tendency, when participating in travel or other potentially risky activities, to cognitively assess threats posed, then respond by performing protective behaviour. We identify travel risks, then make decisions to protect ourselves from them ('I want to see the busy market, but I'll take a tour guide with me'). In the wider field of public health, protection motivation theory predicts that we will follow health advice to prevent threats. For travellers this means avoiding risky destinations and activities, or at least only visiting them with caution (Lu & Wei, 2019). Our ability to protect ourselves is mediated by the level of threat we perceive and by our perceived efficacy for protecting ourselves. Hence, when we think the level of threat associated with travel is manageable, and that it is within our power to minimise those threats, we will go ahead and adopt cautious travel strategies. This may involve travelling locally, delaying a trip, or adopting low risk, socially distanced bubbles (Lu & Wei, 2019; Ruan et al., 2020). Protection motivation theory predicts the type of risk-based travel decisions we will make, leading us to modify our itineraries ('Visiting that place looks risky, so I'll go somewhere else').

But these decisions are more than mere calculations. They are mediated by levels of worry, an additional factor in translating risk perception into protective action (Chien et al., 2017). Worry has been shown to heighten health risk perceptions and so motivate protective behaviour. The more we worry, the more alert we are to travel threats. Worry can be a valuable travel companion. It reminds us of risks and nags us to do something about them (Watkins, 2008).

Although worrying about travel risks prepares us for stressful situations and elicits coping strategies, there are caveats. One of these is the level of control we have over perceived risks. For example, it is helpful to worry about risks that we can do something about, but there is little point in worrying about the uncontrollable or unavoidable. There is a positive correlation between perceived control and protective behavior (Monica Chien et al., 2017), but little point, it seems, in worrying about the heat in Egypt or slipperiness underfoot on a skiing holiday.

Fear, whilst often regarded as a negative emotion, can also help minimise threatening or dangerous travel scenarios. Fear is an emotional response that motivates threat avoidance (Cisler et al., 2009). Like worry, fear prompts protective behaviour in the face of threat (Boss et al., 2015). Whilst fear may be distressing, it helps us take threats more seriously, increasing the likelihood of self-protection (Chen & Yang, 2019). For example, during a global pandemic the threat of travelling to a region with high infection rates can trigger fear, motivating us to protect ourselves by postponing travel. Assisted by fear, worry and any available statistical evidence, we prefer to eliminate risky destinations from our list of alternatives at the travel planning stage (Sharifpour et al., 2014). Evidently, decisions about reducing the risks of travel arise from a combination of emotional responses and rational problem-solving (Zheng et al., 2021).

Much as we try to eliminate triggers for travel fear, sometimes this is beyond us. In travel, as in life, the more in control of a source of danger we are, the less fear we feel (Jonas et al., 2011). The least controllable, most risk-bearing travel threats would include factors such as water quality, food safety, threats of infection. Those we feel moderately in control of (perhaps by having the right equipment or a good map) include avoiding physical or sporting injuries, for example when climbing, walking or swimming. A third group, including sexually transmitted diseases and drug use, are under the control of most travellers (Jonas et al., 2011). Hence, in the face of these variously controllable risks, our self-efficacy is a key factor in the management of travel fear or anxiety. High levels of self-efficacy empower us, prompting us to comply with protective measures and travel advice. There is a positive correlation between perceived efficacy and motivation towards protection (Wang & Ackerman, 2019). The moral here is that if we feel anxious or worried about travel, we should choose an itinerary with more controllable factors, and avoid those that are uncontrollable. The practice of tweaking travel plans by altering routes or avoiding dangerous spaces in order to reduce travel fear is an example of what has been termed *problem-focused coping* (Shimazu & Schaufeli, 2007). In other words, we manage travel risks by deliberate, effective planning. When matters are beyond our control, or where sources of travel fear lie in some past experience that cannot be reversed, we might engage in *emotion-focused coping*. This may involve seeking to regulate our emotions, learning to cope with fears by participating in therapy, mindfulness or some other psychological training.

A therapeutic intervention for reducing phobic and trauma based responses to a travel threat was used with people who had been affected by the 2005 London public transport bombings. Survivors of the bombings were helped to revisit, following counselling, places and forms of transport of which they were fearful. Using this strategy, someone with a fear of travelling by train might be escorted on a railway journey to help them face their fear (Choy et al., 2007). Survivors of the London bombings were given cognitive therapy for PTSD (Ehlers et al., 2005). Cognitive behavioural therapy (CBT) uses techniques such as cognitive restructuring, relaxation and anxiety management. This may involve presenting relevant imagery and describing details of an event or set of events, in order to restructure cognitions. Invasive thoughts ('*I'm never travelling on a train again*') can be replaced, with practice, with more positive ones ('*The likelihood of an attack on public transport is very small'*). In some cases, this technique has enabled people to return to their preferred transport modes with minimal symptoms. Subsequent use of CBT trials has also produced positive results in relation to trauma-based travel phobia (de Jongh et al., 2011). In other, rarer instances, it has had the unwanted consequence of increasing fear responses (Handley et al., 2009).

How curious that an activity such as travel, which most people view as pleasurable or privileged, presents so many challenges. During this chapter we have tried to identify some of these challenges and some strategies for coping with them. Evidently, leaving our zone of comfort, entering the unknown, can be an unsettling as well as stimulating experience.

5

HEDONISM AND SELF-IMPROVEMENT: HOW DOES TRAVEL MAKE US HAPPIER?

FUN AND FULFILMENT

The French philosopher Albert Camus (1995) noted travel's capacity to bring pleasure, but also to test the spirit. Whether we are travelling for pleasure, work, social, religious or health reasons or indeed to test ourselves in some way, we generally do so in the hope that it will make us happier. The happiness travel affords can take various forms, including pure visceral pleasure, peace and quiet or self-improvement. We can travel in pursuit of fun on the beach or ski-slopes, or seek fulfillment and self-improvement at a pilgrimage, spa or language retreat, where healing and learning are more important than fun (Kay Smith & Diekmann, 2017). We can even gain fulfilment from traveling to trace our ancestry and find out who we really are (Nawijn & Filep, 2016). Travel happiness can take many forms and can have as much to do with addressing anxiety as it does the pursuit of pleasure. For some, the happiness afforded by travel is all about getting away from it all; 'it' being work, the daily existential challenge or negative life events (Fu et al., 2015). A change of air can bring psychological restoration or reinvigorate our sense of fascination with the world (Packer, 2008). Temporary physical and mental removal from our everyday environment can restore the spirit, perhaps following a visit to a so-called natural environment (Packer,

DOI: 10.4324/9781003215530-5

2008), or by participating in cultural events, in theatres, museums or in the streets (Pearce et al., 2011). Whether we are on the beach, off the beaten track or wandering round an art gallery, proponents of humanistic or positive psychology argue that there are two main varieties of travel-related wellbeing (Seligman, 2002; Pearce et al., 2011).

The first of these, hedonistic wellbeing, is all about fun and enjoyment. The second, eudemonic wellbeing, involves fulfilment, purpose, or personal development, often acquired over time. Whilst hedonism is associated with pleasure, eudemonic wellbeing relates more to happiness. Hedonic wellbeing is gleaned from the anticipation, experience or memory of sensory pleasures like eating, drinking, swimming or other physical exertions that avail themselves during travel (Ryan & Deci, 2001). Skiing down a mountain, swimming in a lake, eating exotic food, even shopping, exemplify the hedonic pleasures that travel can offer. The pursuit of eudemonic wellbeing follows a more sedate itinerary. It involves experiences that enrich our lives by teaching us something about the world or enhancing our personal qualities. Volunteering abroad, learning a language, visiting an art gallery, even negotiating an unfamiliar transport system, might all yield this more enriching, less euphoric, form of happiness. Personal qualities such as love of learning, appreciation of beauty, creativity, persistence, kindness and resilience can all be enriched by eudemonic travel experiences (Peterson & Seligman, 2004). Arguably, learning and growing through operating outside one's comfort zone reflects the educational role that the 'university of travel' can sometimes have (Pearce & Foster, 2007).

GOING WITH THE FLOW: ENJOYING THE TRAVEL MOMENT

Extreme sports, sun, sea and fun come with the promise of hedonistic pleasure. Whether they deliver on this promise depends on our level of expectation, as well as on the quality of the experience (de Botton, 2014). A spectacular sunset that exceeds expectation is likely to be more pleasurable than one which is just like we imagined it would be. Enhanced wellbeing derived from travel often depends on whether expectations have been met or exceeded (Pearce et al., 2011). This maxim can equally be applied to hedonistic or eudemonic travel. Hence, in answer to the question 'Does travel enhance wellbeing in the short or long term?' we can say 'Yes, when it is better than we thought it would be'.

However, this so-called discrepancy model for linking travel and wellbeing only really works where we have expectations in the first place. This is not always the case. Expectations can be sketchy or even absent altogether (Pearce et al., 2011). This is especially the case when we don't know very much about the place we are visiting. Sometimes, wellbeing during travel can be evaluated minus expectation or subsequent reflection, in the here and now, or immediately afterwards (Pearce, 2005). Shorn of expectations or time for reflection, how we feel about a travel experience often comes down to an immediate response to a lived, felt moment. ('How does this feel right now?'). Arguably too, tapping into how we feel about an experience at the time offers a truer reflection of travel happiness. The ability to let go, forget expectations and comparisons and enjoy the travel moment requires us to go with the flow of fragmentary images and bodily sensations as they are experienced, paying attention to events as they happen (Csikszentmihalyi, 1990). This way of evaluating wellbeing is a far cry from carefully composing a retrospective review on TripAdvisor. It is more of an emotional than a rational reflection. The momentary satisfaction of dancing until dawn, climbing a mountain or watching a sunrise is qualitatively different from calmly weighing up the pros and cons of a hotel or visitor attraction, formulating judgements and awarding five stars. A traveller who is immersed in an activity experiences the world through the body and senses, sometimes with a warped sense of time. Moments are stretched or compressed (Moscardo, 2009). The immersed traveller is willfully distracted. S/he is wooed by new surroundings and does not always think in straight lines. To help us understand the immersive joys of momentary travel experience we can use two influential concepts from positive psychology: mindfulness and flow.

Mindfulness is a desirable state reflecting how we experience the world at a particular moment in time. It affords moment-to-moment awareness of an experience, without judgment (Pearce et al., 2011). Many people aspire to develop mindfulness in everyday life by learning the meditative skill of directing attention, without judgement or evaluation, to their surroundings or inner state of mind. Meditative techniques like yoga and breath control can help with this. A key quality of mindfulness is a capacity to direct attention towards the external and internal world without exercising judgement ('This is how I feel right now, and that's ok'). The mindful individual notices what is happening internally and externally, without recourse to evaluation (Carson & Langer, 2006). The ability to mindfully direct attention towards the present is associated with enhanced wellbeing (Pearce et al., 2011). People who practice mindfulness are found to be significantly more likely to experience eudemonic wellbeing (Garland et al., 2015; George et al., 2021), suggesting a connection between mindful travel and self-improvement. At a mundane level, mindfulness is a handy trick to have up your sleeve when travelling, especially when dealing with delays, detours and interruptions that can sometimes frustrate the hell out of you.

The state of mindfulness is a desirable travel destination. After all, when travelling we constantly experience new environments and to fully appreciate them, it is better to be receptive and mindful, observing new places and our responses to them, without leaping to conclusions too early. Mindfulness involves patience and the ability to extract the good bits of even the most unpromising of locations. It opens travelers to new experiences and has been associated with enhanced satisfaction, effective learning and heightened wellbeing (Carson & Langer, 2006; Moscardo, 2009). The mindful traveller observes without hasty judgement. S/he has the happy knack of identifying pleasure in mundane places (an undiscovered corner, a curious photo opportunity, an unusual soundscape, an unpromising café, an idiosyncratic street sign, an incongruous graffito, a stray cat). One of our main motivations for leisure, recreational or spiritual travel is the pursuit of transformative, memorable moments which are better detected by those with a mindful outlook. Optimum travel moments and associated feelings of wellbeing have been likened to the experience of being in a dance. In both, perception of time is altered, tension is momentarily suspended and awareness of the present is heightened. Such mindful travel moments have been reported by participants in Cuban and Haitian tourist dance practices who entered

> a liminal world that gives relief from day-to-day, ordinary tensions, and, for Cuban dancers and dancing tourists particularly, permits indulgence in near ecstatic experiences.
>
> (Daniel, 1996: 789)

Besides mindfulness, another concept from positive psychology that has been deployed to help us understand how travel can enhance wellbeing in the present moment is flow (Csikszentmihalyi, 1990; Jackson & Eklund, 2004). Whereas mindfulness affords heightened physical and psychological awareness, flow involves absorption in a task or experience, such that awareness recedes. In a flow state we are transported (whether travelling or not) out of ourselves, away from conscious awareness. Flow involves losing yourself in an act (walking, climbing, swimming, praying, gardening, painting, writing) and brings a deep sense of engagement and satisfaction (Csikszentmihalyi, 1990). Originally used to describe feelings experienced by creative artists, this combination of intense engagement, joy and pleasure can also be experienced when visiting new places. A travel flow state reflects immersive engagement with an activity or place, such that we almost lose our sense of separation or identity (Csikszentmihalyi, 1990), as one traveller reports here

> My mind isn't wandering. I am not thinking of something else. I am totally involved in what I am doing. My body feels great. I don't seem to hear anything. The world seems to be cut off from me. I am less aware of myself and my problems.
>
> (Csikszentmihalyi, 1982: 23)

A study into whitewater rafting tourism highlights the link between flow and travel (Wu & Liang, 2011). Rafting – and, by implication, other absorbing activities – enables travellers to actively, physically and psychologically engage with natural or man-made environments. Flow theory can help us understand how travellers are motivated towards certain activities and how participation enhances feelings of wellbeing. An activity such as whitewater rafting affords opportunities for eudemonic skill enhancement, the challenge of succeeding and learning, as well as a sense of playfulness. This combination

> significantly and positively influences tourist flow experience that, in turn, promotes a positive mood and satisfaction.
>
> (Wu & Liang, 2011: 317)

Travel flow is typically experienced during absorbing activities such as windsurfing (Voelkl & Ellis, 1998) or others requiring immersion, challenge and skill development. Climbing, language-learning, art appreciation, skiing or water sports can be both fun and immersive, with the added advantage of helping us learn new skills (Ryan, 1995; Pearce et al., 2011). Flow can be likened to what humanist psychologist Abraham H. Maslow (1954) calls peak experience. We sometimes encounter such moments along journeys towards self-improvement. They simultaneously reflect satisfaction and skill development and are aptly illustrated by eudemonic travel experiences. A study of tourists in flamenco dance workshops (Matteucci & Filep, 2017) highlighted corporeal and sensory aspects of a flow state combining kinaesthetic, haptic, auditory, gustatory, olfactory and visual elements. The immediate satisfaction brought about by absorption in peak experience can be associated with an uplift in mood and wellbeing, feelings of calm, tranquility, with time seemingly being suspended. Intrinsically rewarding experiences are fully engaging and teach us something new, enhancing eudemonic wellbeing. Whilst flow is often associated with active pursuits, less strenuous practices (viewing art, learning a language, cooking) are also flow-inducing, especially when accompanied by the development of expertise, such as learning about an artwork or a place (Ryan, 1995).

Although flow states, being fleeting and at times unexpected, are difficult to monitor, this has been attempted by psychologists who ask participants to record moment-to-moment responses to travel experiences, reporting their dominant thoughts and feelings. This technique is known as event sampling (Csikszentmihalyi, 1990). One study explored flow states in Australian study-abroad students living in Spain (Filep, 2007), with the aim of exploring travellers' micro experiences, thoughts and feelings (Pearce et al., 2011). After sight-seeing at local attractions, interviews were carried out and analysed in order to identify on-the-spot responses. There was evidence of mind-fulness and flow, with travellers reported actively processing what they saw, whilst at the same time learning something from the experience. Some travellers were evidently caught up in peak experience, for example when visiting a museum and accumulating knowledge about history and culture. One participant reported his reaction after seeing Picasso's (1937) Guernica painting in Madrid, which depicts the tragedies and suffering that war inflicts. He described a mixture of challenge, learning and being lost in the moment

> I guess the closest thing I can think of is seeing Picasso's Guernica. That was really one of those things that I was so in awe of that I didn't feel anything for a couple of seconds.

> (Pearce et al., 2011: 55)

Another study, this time conducted with Hungarian tourists, elicited reports of flow-state experience. Participants felt totally involved in a highly rewarding travel activity (Michalkó et al., 2014). Numerous aspects of flow were identified, including the element of challenge, intense awareness of actions, high concentration levels and control, losing self-consciousness, time perception being affected and intrinsic satisfaction. Flow experience has also been observed amongst spa visitors in India, Thailand, and the Philippines (Panchal, 2012).

Mindfulness and flow are overlapping, yet distinct concepts. Both reflect forms of high engagement and the accumulation of knowledge or skills. They are also fluid, intermittent states that can vary in magnitude within the same experience (Filep & Laing, 2019). A key difference between the two is that mindfulness incorporates a greater awareness of the psychological and physical state, without judgement. The latter reflects a greater degree of absorption in the moment. Both states enable us to engage profoundly in travel experiences whilst learning something new. Both are therefore consonant with eudemonic wellbeing (Garland et al., 2015; George et al., 2021), where the emphasis is on enrichment. This is not to say that hedonic pleasure cannot also be derived from activities that are practised mindfully (George et al., 2021). Going with the flow can deliver heightened wellbeing that might combine immediate pleasure (hedonic) with something more eudemonic. The flamenco dancer is both learning, accumulating knowledge (eudemonic), and experiencing pure (hedonic) pleasure (having fun). The fluidity of wellbeing during travel is highlighted too when we consider that that travel wellness can be hedonic and eudemonic at different times within the same excursion (Voigt, 2010), at different times within the same dance.

Travel satisfaction is a mixture of positive evaluations in the form of feelings and cognitions. These are sometimes experienced immediately, sometimes in retrospect, in a more reflective form. Mindfulness and flow can help us understand how we appreciate these moments on-the-go. Broadly speaking, engaging in a challenging but doable, absorbing travel activity which enhances our skillset is associated with mindfulness and flow, and appears to enhance eudemonic wellbeing. Furthermore, dynamic, creative activities which promote flow have been seen to improve wellbeing more than passive activities such as lying on a beach or scrolling through social media (Schiffer & Roberts, 2018). There is a travel paradox here too. Despite the greater degree of reported wellbeing or self-improvement associated with effortful, enriching activities, people are often drawn towards more passive travel 'inactivities', partly because they require less effort (Schiffer & Roberts, 2018). Sometimes, the attraction of sedentary relaxation outweighs the more effortful investment of personal enrichment.

After all, for many people, travel represents a well-earned break from self-improvement, and a rare opportunity to be passive.

TIME, TRAVEL AND WELLBEING

William James (1890), one of psychology's founding figures, was one of the first to write about the distorting effect that enjoyable experience has on time perception. He noted that hours happily spent are often perceived as relatively short in duration, and yet are recalled fondly and at greater length. Flow theorist Csikszentmihalyi (1990) also noticed the perceived acceleration of time during absorbing activities. Conversely, time spent doing nothing much can appear to drag and is barely recalled. We regularly relive and recall our favorite travel experiences (walks, parties, excursions) at great length, elongating them in the telling, whilst skipping the details of those hours spent queuing, transferring, making reservations, waiting around in hotel lobbies and airport lounges. During mundane travel experiences the hours pass slowly since they are free of fun and distraction (Levine, 1997).

Despite these generalities, it has also been suggested that the relationship between time perception and travel affects different people in different ways (Pearce et al., 2011). Individual differences in time perception orientation have been reported (Zimbardo, 2002). During travel (and other activities) some people focus more on the here and now whilst others tend to have one eye on the future. At one end of this continuum, those with a so-called present-time orientation (living in the present, going with the flow) have a higher propensity to engage in travel involving hedonism, high risk extreme sports, getting lost in the moment, short-term sexual encounters, drugs and alcohol use (Keogh et al., 1999). These travellers are more likely to perceive time as accelerating during absorbing activities. They are also less likely to book or plan travel itineraries in advance (or buy travel insurance). Contrastingly, those with a future-time orientation (planners who are less consumed by the here and now) are less prone to losing themselves in the flow of pleasurable activity. Travel choices and enjoyment levels may be mediated by individual differences in time perception orientation (Argyle, 2002). A person with a future-time orientation typically favours cautious, organised, low risk itineraries. They find it harder to let go, take risks or stop thinking about responsibilities back home. They struggle to enjoy the moment; being more concerned with planning ahead and setting goals.

The best travel advice that this theory can offer is to find a happy medium between present and future orientations (Zimbardo (2002). Arguably, the secret of enjoyable travel is flexibility; being able to flip between present and future orientations as circumstance demands. For example, it may be best to adopt a present-time orientation whilst participating in activities such as skiing, walking or visiting galleries, and a future-time orientation whilst planning the excursion beforehand. An overactive future time orientation can dilute the experience of a swim, gallery visit or walk. An overactive present orientation hampers the capacity to plan a journey and get the logistics right. Someone with a balanced perspective is more likely to immerse themselves in a visit to a monument, or a coastal walk, even where this activity is not likely to contribute to increasing their income in the future (Pearce et al., 2011).

> Visitation to a historic site, for example, may be more satisfying and be associated with greater levels of overall wellbeing if the person had the opportunity to reach a balanced time perspective.
>
> (Pearce et al., 2011: 68)

Just as travel happiness is likely to be derived from a mixture of hedonistic and eudemonic travel activities, a flexible balance between absorption in the present and concern for the future seems to make for happier travel.

DOES TRAVEL HAVE A LASTING EFFECT ON WELLBEING?

During this chapter we have seen how positive and humanistic psychology have explored the relationship between wellbeing and travel as it is experienced, using concepts such as flow, mindfulness and time perception orientation. But what about the emotional and psychological impressions that travel leaves on us when we return home? If travel makes us happy whilst we're doing it, does the effect last through the days, weeks and months after our homecoming? Arguably, the tourism industry is primarily concerned with promoting short-term happiness. It is less bothered about bringing long term, lasting meaning to our lives (Nawijn, 2011). However, the extent to which psychological wellbeing stays with us has drawn the interest of psychologists. Some studies reveal post-holiday improvements in mood (Chen & Petrick, 2013), whilst others suggest a travel hangover – a dip in wellbeing amongst those returning from travel (Kirillova & Lehto, 2015). There are reports of holidays with longer-lasting positive outcomes for wellbeing and life satisfaction, specifically when participants also report that travel is something that is important to them (Uysal et al., 2016). The age of a traveler can also be a mediating factor for long-term, post-travel satisfaction. More mature travellers report higher levels of wellbeing more than two months after returning from a holiday, with the additional benefit of having fewer health visits and doses of medication during the same period. A gender gap has also been identified, with females reporting more temporary effects of increased wellbeing after a holiday. They also reported higher stress levels prior to travel than men did (Nawijn et al., 2013), with the burden of organisation disproportionately falling on them. The lasting positive effects of travel on romantic relationships have also been studied, using psychometrics and telephone interviews (Laing & Frost, 2017). Participants claimed to be generally happier than normal during a holiday, experiencing more meaningful interactions and higher satisfaction levels in their relationship. Sadly, this tailed off soon after returning home. Whilst there may be no guarantee of a travel boost for a relationship, it has been argued that the happiness and meaning derived from travel depends not just on the places we visit, but also on the relationships we foster whilst travelling (Packer & Gill, 2017). In other words, travel is not just about sightseeing. It is also an opportunity for sharing experiences, developing teamwork and having deep conversations, all of which can be achieved in the context of a shared travel experience (De Bloom et al., 2017).

The mixed evidence reported here suggests that long-term effects of travel may be negligible even if travel does heighten positive emotions at the time (Mitas et al., 2017). Most studies show that hedonic wellbeing declines fairly rapidly post-excursion (Filep & Laing, 2019). Interviewing Dutch participants before and after they returned from their holidays, little or no difference in happiness was found when travellers were compared with those who stayed at home (Nawijn et al., 2013). A short-term travel effect was identified in another study where health and wellbeing were seen to rise during a holiday, but not to persist (De Bloom et al., 2017). Such fadeout effects suggest that the pleasure we derive from travel often offers little more than a temporary respite from existential anxieties (De Botton, 2014). This said, in relation to the difference between hedonic and eudemonic travel, it is also suggested that the latter can provide a longer-term tonic for the existential spirit (Kirillova & Lehto, 2015). The effect of art appreciation or learning a new skill seemingly stays with us for longer than the visceral pleasures of hedonistic travel.

Can we reduce the fadeout effect after an enjoyable travel experience? Arguably, the best way to prolong travel's positive effects is to learn how to savour it (Tugade & Fredrickson, 2004).

> Savouring prolongs the duration of positive emotional experiences when thinking about the imminent arrival at a destination (anticipation), when savouring pleasurable moments (on-site experiences), and when relishing memories upon return to usual domiciles (reflection).
>
> (Filep & Laing, 2019: 349)

Savouring positive emotions felt during travel (love, interest, joy, contentment) sustains enhanced wellbeing before a trip (anticipation), during (appreciation) and afterwards (reflection and reminiscence). One study explored how Chinese independent tourists actively savoured their travels using travel blogs. They consciously extended their positive reflections through creating online narratives to keep the good feelings alive (Filep & Laing, 2019). Specifically, it was found that the most savoured experiences were those related to being in natural, green or coastal places. Perhaps one way of extending the positive effects of our travels on our wellbeing is to actively recall, record and retell the stories we accumulate, using word of mouth, photographs, travelogues, diaries, social media, even by going back to writing postcards.

In this chapter we have learned of the differing forms of wellbeing that travel affords, from the instant joy of hedonistic pleasure to the more considered, eudemonic happiness we get from learning new skills and improving ourselves. Whilst both these forms of happiness can be experienced in the moment, using flow and mindfulness, we have also seen how some of us find it easier to enjoy travel experiences in the moment. Others are more oriented towards the future, and so find it harder to let go. Can we generate any travel advice from this short exploration of travel and wellbeing? Perhaps the best way to achieve travel happiness is to pack in a healthy dose of hedonism alongside the pursuit of self-improvement, to live in the moment during those special moments of peak experience and then to savour these journeys by writing postcards, posting photographs and telling tales.

6

UNFORGETTABLE JOURNEYS: NOSTALGIA, HOMESICKNESS AND OTHER TRAVEL MEMORIES

THE BEST BITS OF OUR LIVES: WHY IS TRAVEL SO MEMORABLE?

The times we spend travelling are amongst the most memorable. For most people travel is a departure from everyday life, so it stays in the memory for longer. Unusual, extraordinary travel experiences are especially memorable. They create so-called flashbulb memories: exceptional, vivid, long lasting memories of surprising events (Kim, 2010). Travel is especially conducive to creating flashbulb memories because it is a distinctive category of experience. It has been described as "a temporary no-work, no-care, no-thrift situation" (Cohen, 1979: 181). Even work-related travel is usually distinctive. For those of us who spend most of our time living in one place, travel facilitates the suspension of quotidian routines, it offers excitement and unpredictability and memories are made of this.

Travelling is especially memorable because it involves novel encounters in unfamiliar places. These encounters offer us a chance to see ourselves anew, to refresh our image of who we are. The travelling self experiences newness and jeopardy that our sedentary self rarely encounters. On our travels we see ourselves in testing circumstances and find

DOI: 10.4324/9781003215530-6

out how we cope without home comforts. Put to the test in a new city or in a different culture, we see ourselves reflected in the eyes of those who meet us for the first time. Travel experiences may be memorable because they enliven and challenge our sense of identity, our so-called existential authenticity (Wang, 2000). This feeling of existential authenticity is more immediate when we are away from everyday constraints. We commit this image of our travelling selves to memory ('I remember how I coped when I was alone in X for the first time'). Our existential authenticity is activated by memorable, unusual encounters (meeting new people, negotiating unfamiliar situations, speaking a different language). Travel experiences are existentially testing. They reveal a subjective feeling of vitality, showing a different self under testing conditions (Cohen, 1979). Fragments of these moments of authenticity form unforgettable travel stories and are sometimes remembered as the best bits of our lives.

The more immersed we are in a travel experience, the more deeply involved at a cognitive level, the more challenged we feel, the stronger and longer lasting our travel memories are. Tourists have noted that they recall their experiences of a place better when they are more immersed in activities there (Kim, 2010). This suggests that doing something in a new place is more memorable than merely seeing it as a sightseer, or when merely passing through on a flying visit. Deeper immersion and involvement in local cultural activities enhances travel memory and heightens powers of recollection. Interacting with local cultures and local people produces unique, memorable travel experiences (Morgan & Xu, 2009). Travel, as an interruption to daily routine, is inherently memorable, especially in the presence of active immersion in and emotional bonding with new places or cultures.

NOSTALGIA AND HOMESICKNESS

> You can't go home again because home has ceased to exist except in the mothballs of memory.
>
> Steinbeck (1960), *Travels with Charley*

Although it is inherently memorable, travel also has the capacity to generate melancholy memories. Sometimes travel makes us feel sad, especially when we are far from home and thinking of where we came from. Two different varieties of travel sadness have passed into everyday discourse. But how do *homesickness* and *nostalgia* differ? The Oxford English Dictionary (2016) defines homesickness as

> sadness caused by the longing for home or family during a period of absence.

Nostalgia is defined as

> sentimental longing for, or regretful memory of, a place or period from one's past.

A notable difference between these two types of sadness is that home-sickness is a little less severe and might be remedied by returning home for a soothing spell of personal memory tourism: a reacquaintance with home (Morse & Mudgett, 2017). Meanwhile, the melancholy associated with nostalgia is harder to overcome. This is a longing for past times and places which are sometimes irretrievable. A nostalgic person misses people and places (houses, gardens, neighbourhoods, social networks) from earlier life stages. Nostalgia resonates with the travel experiences of groups such as soldiers and migrants (Sedikides et al., 2008). Psychoanalysts have even labelled nostalgia as 'immi-grant psychosis' (Frost, 1938). Experienced as an emotional memo-rial response, nostalgia is an affectively charged yearning for episodes from our autobiographical memory (Verplanken, 2012; Madoglou et al., 2017). Sometimes this takes the form of actively exploring the past by evoking memories deliberately, such as scrolling through old photographs (Howard, 2012). At other times it is unplanned, when involuntary autobiographical memories invade the consciousness.

Nostalgia entered our vocabulary around 1688 when the physician Johannes Hofer diagnosed it as

> a sad mood originating from the desire for the return to one's native land.

(Hofer, 1934: 382)

Typical symptoms of this new melancholic condition were invasive memories of home or of familiar, unattainable places and people. In one of Hofer's case studies a young Swiss student from Berne became ill when away from home, only to recover as soon as he began his return journey. According to modern definitions the effectiveness of this strategy for reducing sadness fits better with the notion of homesickness (Morse & Mudgett, 2017). In later writings, the term nostalgia was more commonly reserved for those who had wandered far from home and presented psychological and physical symptoms such as sadness, poor appetite, or inconsolability. For the hopeless nostalgic, a remedy based on travelling home was either unavailable or ineffective. In the 19th century, when psychology itself was still emerging, the symptoms of nostalgia were seen as being aggravated by associative thinking during travel (recalling home). Memories were jogged by physical landmarks, familiar sounds, evocative aromas, all of which could arouse melancholia. In some cases, therapists even treated invasive, associative nostalgia by recommending shutting off unhealthy memories of home. This cast nostalgic travellers as rather tragic, isolated figures.

In both mild cases of homesickness and more serious cases of nostalgia, the traveller misses previously known people and places. Fond, invasive memories of physical landscapes and social networks contribute to feelings of homesickness and nostalgia. Both varieties of travel sadness have physical, social and temporal dimensions. We miss places, people and times. Today we might regard homesickness and nostalgia less as illnesses, more as understandable expressions of place attachment (Morse & Mudgett, 2017) reflecting an

> affective bond developed by people with a place over time.
>
> (Steg et al., 2013: 105)

When we are 'place-attached', emotionally linked to physical and social aspects of somewhere such as a hometown, it is understandable that remembering them from afar can make us feel sad. Research amongst Appalachian migrants suggests that what we miss is people as well as physical spaces (Barcus & Brunn, 2010). Furthermore, homesickness and nostalgia are not just experienced in relation to homes, families, houses or private spaces. These feelings can also extend to public spaces and streets. Research conducted in Vermont (U.S.) reported a deeper attachment to aspects of the state landscape than to privately owned property and land (Morse & Mudgett, 2017). It appears that when travellers confess to missing home, they are expressing a yearning for more than merely a dwelling. What they are missing extends to their social networks, familiar neighbourhood spaces which, as they are recalled fondly, constitute a central part of the self.

Sometimes the best remedy for homesickness is a return ticket. Going home partially relieves the homesick traveller. Whilst temporal aspects of home may be irretrievable ('*so many things have changed since I was last here*'), some of we leave behind may still be there. We can go home physically, step off a train and ease our feelings of homesickness. To an extent, we can even do so virtually, using photographs, video conferencing or social media, hopefully finding that things haven't changed all that much.

> It is possible to assuage environmental homesickness with a trip home, and these trips home, whether in-person visits, or checking on events, images, and people back home through social media, may help leavers maintain their place-based identities.
>
> (Morse & Mudgett, 2017: 101)

Homesickness and nostalgia are both associated with travelling away from home. Places, times and people we miss can provoke feelings of sadness which might be assuaged by returning home, even if what we find when we get there is much altered.

ARRIVAL STORIES: USING MEMORY TO MAKE SENSE OF NEWLY ENCOUNTERED PLACES

Travel memory isn't all about sadness, loss and longing. Besides reminding us of where we came from, memory helps us to make sense of the places we discover as we travel. Remembering is more than just delving into the past. It provides us with a means of understanding the present. Place attachment theory asserts that memories of where we grow up are more than just a series of fading, distant recollections. They are a vibrant part of who we are. They affirm our connections with people and places and stay with us no matter how far, or for how long, we wander (Scannell & Gifford, 2010). As we travel these affective bonds influence how we make sense of places we come across, enabling us to attach meanings to newly discovered places (Altman & Low, 1992).

Memories associated with place attachments evoke the past, but they also propel us forward, towards new experiences. For example, when first arriving in a new city, perceptions of its odd-looking features (novel street signs, shopfronts, customs, language, terrain) are influenced by customs, language and street signs remembered from home. In one case study, migrants arriving in Manchester (England) from Indonesia, Spain, Germany, Romania, Zambia and Tunisia were accompanied around their new city and interviewed about how they made sense of these surroundings (Stevenson, 2014). These migrants from diverse locations converged on the same location simultaneously. They used their sensory memories (vision, sound, touch, olfaction) to help them make sense of their new surroundings. We encounter new places through the immediacy of sight, touch, sound and olfaction, and our responses are partly dictated by sensations we remember from home. Whether wandering through a newly encountered market, visiting a new building or being invited into someone's home in a newly discovered city, we navigate similarity and difference using our memories and senses. We may be transported home by a familiar smell or by a taste from our past (coffee, soap, flowers). Memorable tastes, smells and sounds can transport the traveller home momentarily, reaffirming place attachments, offering ways of gauging how similar or different a new place feels and how comfortable one feels there. A familiar food encountered in a new place, for example, helps us to revive intense memories, to recall places or past times. An everyday habit with an accompanying aroma (morning coffee, sizzling fish) can recreate past times of sociality and belonging (Sutton, 2001), making us feel better about a new place since it links us with our past. A sort of gustatory nostalgia surfaces in the displaced person who visits evocative sectors of a new city (Mankekar, 2002).

Besides smell and taste, travellers also use sonic memory to build connections between past and present. Sounds of running water, birdsong, or the call of a street vendor, can connect us to past experiences or momentarily accentuate the novelty of somewhere new (Diaz, 2007). A series of sonic memories were identified and recorded by a migrant from Indonesia, who, on visiting Manchester for the first time, was reminded of home by the sounds of water fountains and running ornamental streams in the university campus where she was making her new home (Stevenson, 2014). Courtesy of these sonic reminders she became drawn to a series of peaceful locations in her new city; locations that reminded her of Indonesia. Sound-based memories and affective bonds (Drever, 2002) can be revived by visiting locations that link past places with new ones (a beach, a church, a fountain, a garden). These evocative, often personally poignant, sites of memory are emotionally saturated points of reference through which wanderers move and imaginatively make sense of new places though connections with their pasts.

Connections between new and old places are forged by sensory experiences that highlight similarity ('that smell reminds me of my village') and difference ('the noise here is so different from back home'). Memory and place attachment play an orienting role in the process of making sense of newly encountered locations (Rishbeth & Powell, 2013). Tastes, sounds, aromas, even spatial arrangements, can evoke sensorial and corporeal memories of past places ('this square reminds me of the village where I grew up', 'that smell reminds me of our old corner store'). Memory itself, far from being reduced to units of knowledge stored in an internal archive, is a dynamic practice for fashioning narratives that can help us make a smooth transition when trying to get used to a whole new set of challenges. Memory isn't just used to recall old places. It helps us make sense of new ones.

DOING THE KNOWLEDGE: HOW BODIES REMEMBER

Psychologists have long debated where memory is located. Some regard our store of recollections as literally that; an internal archive into which we encode and from which we (hopefully) retrieve knowledge. Hence, like all memories, travel recollections would take their place in such an archive, amongst other fragments of knowledge about our past. They would be registered in what has been theorised as a long-term memory store (Atkinson & Shiffrin, 1968). Subsequently we then retrieve these fragments, episodes and travel anecdotes. Travel itineraries, routes, place names, like all other mnemonic material, are, according to this archival model, learned (registered), encoded (stored), then retrieved, depending on factors such as how well we rehearse the material, the passage of time and so on. The more often we trot out a travel story, rehearsing it in the process, the easier it is to remember, give or take one or two embellishments and omissions.

An alternative way of thinking about human memory, which is especially relevant to travel, is to understand it as a physical practice (something we do) rather than as an internal storage facility (Brockmeier, 2010). For example, it is sometimes said that with the aid of muscle-memory, bodies remember how to drive a car, ride a bicycle or play a sitar. Perhaps travel memory works like this too. The dynamic nature of travel encourages us to see travel memory as part of a physical process that we exercise as we journey around. After all, travel stories are made from places visited, activities practised, routes traced and retraced. Our recollections (*'walking in Paris in the spring', 'filming the desert at night', 'rafting across the Mekong River'*) are narratives that stay with us because we physically lived through them with our bodies and senses. We remember them because they emanate from a process known as living-thinking (Ingold, 2000; Thrift, 2008), rather than from reading, rehearsing or processing information into a long-term store.

The living-thinking approach sees memorable journeys leaving lasting impressions that are inseparable from emplaced, sensory and embodied engagements with real places (walking, getting lost, climbing, skiing). Travel memories are strenuously wrought from the repetitive negotiation of familiar places ('I make this walk every day'), or from novel encounters with new routes or destinations ('I will never forget walking across Helsinki for the first time'). Either way, these recollections are inseparable from physical journeys. They yield their own travel stories, some of which may be more accurate than others, depending on the passage of time, level of immersion or frequency of telling. You could say that lived, emplaced memories, based on strenuous engagement with places (Cresswell, 2004) are akin to what taxi drivers call 'doing the knowledge'. Like taxi drivers who get to know their patch by driving round it repeatedly, we accumulate travel memories through physical and sensory experience. It isn't just cab drivers who do the knowledge. We're all doing it. By accumulating emplaced memories and attachments we gather a form of situated intelligence. This knowledge is inseparable from places and movement. In accumulating situated knowledge, we develop place attachments and attach personal meanings to locations. This process of attaching meanings to locations is known as place-making (Cresswell, 2004). Through place-making we transform mere locations on a map into personally unforgettable places. From the places we make through our embodied travel emerge emplaced memories that are drenched in meaning.

CAN TRAVEL IMPROVE YOUR MEMORY?

Actively engaging with the landscape (walking, running, cycling, swimming, climbing, driving) not only creates meaningful memories, but also revives fading ones. Going back to a previously visited place can bring back earlier experiences. This can be a positive outcome for those with fading recall. There is evidence of a link between physical exercise and memory performance, with walking shown to improve learning and recall (Eisner, 2004). Travel experiences leave traces of muscle memory (Tod et al., 2010) which can be revived on a revisit. Very often our bodies seem to remember the feel of a place re-encountered, as though the initial experience was retained in our musculature (Chaiklin & Wengrower, 2009).

It is extremely evocative to walk along a path from childhood; we draw together aspects of place and biography through the walk.

(Schine, 2010: 4)

As we move through previously experienced landscapes the reactivation of memory further supports the view that memory is something which resides in the body, rather than being hidden away in an internal archival store. The notion of muscle memory, jogged whilst walking or riding, blurs the boundary between mind and body. It suggests that memory is located somewhere between thought, body and place, between cognition, embodiment and environment. As we engage actively with environments knowledge is constructed and memories are made. Mobility can actively bring forth personal biographies and travel stories that sometimes elude the decontextualised introspection of merely sitting and thinking (Lee, 2004).

There may be some therapeutic value in travel which helps us to actively remember earlier biographical detail. Revisiting a place to remember can be valuable for those who are nostalgic, homesick or who may be experiencing memory loss. The evocation of emplaced memories through travel has been explored by reuniting participants with pre-loved memorable places. In one study, revisiting a Scottish village from childhood evoked memory with exceptional detail (Järviluoma, 2009). Several mobile memory projects have demonstrated the benefits of travel for bringing back autobiographical memory. Travel can be a therapeutic exercise, enabling individuals to reflectively interact with space, reviving meaningful relationships with them (Lee, 2004). Dementia studies highlight the value of walking for providing the opportunity to capture lived experiences through movement (Odzakovic et al., 2020). A nostalgic visit can be therapeutic, restoring positive narratives of place (Ye et al., 2017), enhancing feelings of belongingness, growth and identity (Baldwin & Landau, 2014). Revisiting places and memories simultaneously, can enhance and protect the self by reviving life scripts and personal narratives (Sedikides & Wildschut, 2018).

PHOTOGRAPHIC MEMORIES: PRESERVING TRAVEL IN PICTURES

> Memory is the single most important source of information for an individual to decide whether he or she would revisit a location.
>
> (Kim, 2010: 781)

How we remember a place we visit affects our likelihood of revisiting it (Barnes et al., 2016). Memories of satisfying experiences (Madoglou et al., 2017), good customer service (Frochot & Hughes, 2000) or of something out of the ordinary (Stylos et al., 2016), increase the likelihood of a repeat visit. We are more likely to go back to a place when seeking out likeminded people or if we have an emotional bond with it or a desire to re-experience something we are missing (Zhang et al., 2021). The more fondly we recall a place, the deeper the attachment, the more likely we are to go back (Prayag & Lee, 2018).

The tourism industry is in the business of producing memorable experiences for customers in the hope that one day they will come back for more. Travel companies strive to provide 'wow moments' of immersion (a full sensory experience), surprise, (unexpected, unique encounters), participation (actively getting involved) and fun that they hope will linger long in the memory and translate into place attachments and revisit intentions. One study of Taiwanese hotel guests found a positive correlation between the development of place attachments, positive hotel experiences and the intention to go back (Tsai et al., 2020). Tourism is designed to create happy memories and make regular visitors of us all.

Travel photography can help with this. Photographs memorialise 'I was there' moments which we can enjoy and share, producing positive affect that lingers long after the event. They sustain travel narratives about people, places and experiences, for us to record and relive on demand. The deliberate autobiographical memories we store photographically in our albums, mobile devices and on social media also increase the tendency to return to a destination (Zhang et al., 2021). Pleasant travel memories that guide our future decisions are encoded in our long-term memory albums and feeds. Furthermore, the better the quality of the photograph and the more of them there are, the more frequently we view and share them, the more frequently they will arouse autobiographical memories of travel and revisit intentions (Zhang et al., 2021).

Travel photographs are a fun, popular way of marking and reliving moments spent in fondly remembered places. They are a handy archive of deliberately generated autobiographical memories (Zhang et al., 2021). We use photographs to recall our travels and they reward us by evoking positive emotional responses and treasured travel narratives. However, they can also be unreliable. They are an episodic, idiosyncratic version of events (Kim, 2010). Pictures shape and distort the way we see our past travel experiences, allowing us to edit out the bits we would rather forget. As curators of these archives, we create photo-fictions of travel, viewed retrospectively through a rose-tinted tourist gaze (Urry, 1990) that highlights people, landscapes and events that are "exotic", "romantic", "fun", "surprising" or "picturesque", at the expense of the mundane experiences we delete from our memories or don't bother to capture. These partial pictorial travelogues single out what we want to recall and repress unrecorded or unpalatable moments (*'the hours spent waiting at the airport', 'the day we got locked out of our hotel', 'the time it rained all day', 'the boring guy we couldn't get rid of'*). Travel photographs raise the status of some events in memory. They capture moments of heightened positive emotion, rather than providing a CCTV-style, warts and all account of travel experience. As we travel, we often experience the full range of emotions, yet we only tend to document the good bits (Bastiaansen et al., 2019). The selective nature of photographic travel memory is important when deciding whether to go back to a place. After all, the person making the decisions about future travel is the remembering self, not the experiencing self (Kahneman, 2011).

We have seen in this chapter that experiences of travel do not end when we return home. Travel is a memorable, often novel, category of experience and memory sustains our travel narratives, baking them into our personal histories, especially when experiences have been immersive and emotionally charged. Travel is very often unforgettable and emotional, even though sometimes it can make us long for the people and places we leave behind. At times, travel can be made easier because of the wealth of memories we carry with us, helping us to make sense of new places, providing continuity of experience. The experience of visiting different places stimulates memories of home. At the same time, travel creates fresh memories and meanings that stay with us long into the future in the form of internal archives, muscle memories and partially reliable photographic records.

7

CULTURE SHOCKS AND BORDER CROSSINGS: TRAVEL AND INTERCULTURAL ENCOUNTER

An acceleration of travel patterns in the late 20th and early 21st centuries has made the experience of meeting people and ideas from diverse cultures (aka intercultural encounter) far more common for many people. This chapter explores the link between travel and intercultural encounter and specifically the psychological implications of exposure to diversity. Psychologists with an interest in travel and intercultural encounter have deployed three main ideas to advance our understanding: acculturation, biculturalism and cosmopolitanism.

ACCULTURATION: ACCLIMATISING TO DIVERSITY

When we encounter a cultural group for the first time it can take time to adapt and adjust. Meeting people from different places, with diverse traditions, is of course part of the travel experience, whether we are moving across international borders or within them. These intercultural encounters require an adaptation process that is known as *acculturation*. The term derives from the broader concept of culture, which can be defined as a unique way of living, involving attitudes, norms, behaviours and traditions that are shared by a social group (Stevenson, 2020). Many different cultural groups co-exist within national or regional

DOI: 10.4324/9781003215530-7

boundaries, so it is worth noting that culture and nation are not the same thing, despite the prevalence of terms like 'Japanese culture' in everyday conversation (Berry, 2006). Nations generally have within their boundaries several, sometimes hundreds, of cultural groups.

Acculturation happens

> when groups of individuals having different cultures come into continuous first-hand contact, with subsequent changes in the original culture patterns of either or both groups.
>
> (Redfield et al., 1936: 149)

Acculturation is synonymous with travel practices like tourism, migration, international study, involuntary displacement. It goes with the territory in any scenario where people from different cultures mix. It is a reciprocal process, too, affecting both travellers and hosts (Berry et al., 2011). We are incrementally influenced by those we meet on our travels, and travellers have an influence on host communities too. As with all incremental psychological processes (learning, maturation, language acquisition), acculturation is not an all-or-nothing phenomenon. It is perfectly possible to identify with a new culture whilst, to a greater or lesser extent, retaining elements (behaviours, beliefs, values) of one's original culture (Rasmi et al., 2014). Those who travel are drawn to new ways of life whilst simultaneously retaining an identification with what they know.

The idea of acculturation was originally constructed as a group phenomenon, relating to the mixing of neighbouring cultural groups, perhaps as national borders become more porous and social mixing more common. However, we can also understand it at the individual level, using the term psychological acculturation (Graves, 1967). Thus, even within groups who experience acculturation, for example following travel or migration, some individuals will experience it differently. In other words, some of us are influenced more, less or differently, by the people and practices we come across when traveling. Psychological acculturation affects international students, tourists, economic migrants, as well as hosts whose cultural space is populated by visitors. It can be entered into willingly or reluctantly. It can be short term or long term. It can be a positive or negative experience. After all, the acculturation of an international student who travels to another culture is likely to be very different from (and probably more positive than) that of someone who has been forcibly deported. The term acculturative stress refers to the challenges that come with acculturation, for example when asylum seekers and migrants leave their homelands, voluntarily or otherwise, and encounter feelings of rejection, uncertainty or rootlessness (Berry et al., 2011). Acculturative stress was reported in one study with Italian migrants in English-speaking countries, who showed low scores on emotional stability, attachment to their new culture and linguistic inclusion (Panicacci & Dewaele, 2017). In another study, this time exploring host culture perspectives, indigenous populations in Greenland, Russia, Alaska and Norway reported that involuntary contact with people from other cultures correlated with a perceived 'loss of culture' (Eliassen et al., 2012). These sentiments are commonly reported anecdotally by some inhabitants of nation states that experience high levels of immigration. It is worth noting too though that these sentiments are far from universal amongst hosts.

Stressful or not, travel and intercultural encounter, especially over a sustained period, are associated with acculturative changes that are often visible and audible, for example in dress, talk, consumption and social etiquette. Less visibly, they also involve changes in feelings and attitudes. Psychologists have attempted to measure these wide-ranging changes psychometrically (using questionnaires), revealing alterations in levels of wellbeing and self-rated health scores (Sam & Berry, 2010; Panicacci & Dewaele, 2017) following intercultural encounters. Whether these changes are visible to the naked eye (behaviours) or not (attitudes and feelings), we can distinguish between an 'A, B and C' of acculturation; affect, behaviour and cognition.

Affective acculturation is an emotional response to new cultural experiences. Changing a culture of residence requires a period of adjustment and adaptation to a different set of emotional expectations. Prolonged emotional readjustment has been observed in several first-generation migrant groups, such as Koreans in the U.S. and Turkish migrants in Belgium (De Leersnyder, 2017). Unsurprisingly perhaps, in both groups, the acquisition of emotional responses that were conventional in host cultures was made easier where migrants were able to engage more in relationships with their hosts (De Leersnyder et al., 2011). Behavioural acculturation occurs when cultural transition requires the learning of new behavioral repertoires (Berry et al., 2011), such as norms of greetings, personal space, joking and eating. This means acquiring novel behavioural responses to help navigate the choppy cross-cultural waters that characterise differences in social etiquette (Ward et al., 2010). For example, newly arrived international students face a host of different customs (for example, norms relating to punctuality) when arriving in a new country, adding to the existing academic challenge of studying in a second language. One study found that amongst some cohorts of international students, the learning of new behavioural norms was eased by engagement with new media platforms, such as host TV channels, and by participation in social media groups with new acquaintances from host cultures (Yu et al., 2019). Cognitive acculturation requires changes in decision-making and the processing of new information during intercultural encounter. Living in a new country, for example, might require thinking differently about in-group or out-group membership ('*Am I a resident or a visitor?*') or rethinking cognitions about belongingness (Tajfel & Turner, 1979). Many people need to feel they belong to a group (national, cultural, occupational) in order to feel happy, since definitions such as 'national', 'resident', 'visitor' can impact wellbeing. Long-term travel or changes in cultural circumstances can challenge these appraisals, affecting our sense of who we are (Berry et al., 2011), perhaps even leading to a feeling of identity confusion. These affective, behaviour and cognitive adaptations are all interrelated, and really amount to a bundle of changes that influence how intercultural encounter makes us feel, act and think.

Movement between cultures requires a period of readjustment and acclimatisation. Psychologists refer to this process, which involves adaptations in behaviour, attitudes and emotion, as psychological acculturation. This period of acclimatisation is likely to be temporary, and, with increased contact, is likely to become less stressful over time. However, there is no single, catch-all strategy for acculturating. Different people do it differently.

DILEMMAS OF ASSIMILATION, SEPARATION, INTEGRATION AND MARGINALISATION

The effectiveness of different strategies for adapting to intercultural encounter rests on two 'push-pull' factors (Nguyen & Benet-Martínez, 2013). The first of these relates to maintenance ('*How much do I want to maintain my own cultural heritage when I meet new people?*'), whilst the second relates to integration (*How important is it for me to integrate into another culture?*). During acculturation these dilemmas play out in multiple areas of life, such as language, food, dress, beliefs and attitudes. Essentially, the acculturating traveller must decide whether to get involved in all, some, or no newly encountered cultural practices.

Using this integration-maintenance dilemma as a guide, Berry et al. (2011) outline four common acculturation strategies that travellers typically adopt, with each one representing a different level of engagement and participation. The first strategy, known as *assimilation*, involves rejecting or moving away from one's own cultural identity by adopting the values, beliefs and norms of another, newly encountered culture ('*I embrace the new culture wholeheartedly and am prepared to change the way I eat and dress*'). Strategy two, *separation*, is a rejection of the values, beliefs and norms of a newly encountered culture in favour of retaining one's own cultural heritage ('*I'll continue to dress, eat and talk as I always have, even in another country*'). The third strategy, *integration*, represents a middle ground, and involves simultaneously retaining aspects of one's own culture whilst engaging with aspects of a newly encountered one ('*Whilst retaining a lot of my cultural traditions, I still want to sample the food, music and customs of this new place, so I'll mix and match*'). Finally, *marginalisation* involves backing away both from one's own cultural heritage and the values, beliefs and norms of a newly encountered culture ('*I reject cultural influence and just be myself*').

In an overview of the acculturation literature, Berry et al. (2011) identify integration as the most popular strategy amongst travellers. Marginalisation was the least common. However, these tactics are not mutually exclusive. At various times we may dip in and out of each of the strategies, depending on the nature of the intercultural encounter we are involved in (e.g. tourism, international study, migration), or even on our mood. Some days we just don't feel like integrating and prefer to be alone. These strategies are patterns of behaviour which reflect attraction, rejection or indifference towards newly encountered cultures. They vary across, within individuals and groups, and over time. For example, one Scandinavian study found Finnish adolescents to mellow with age, becoming more integrationist, less assimilationist (Nshom & Croucher, 2018). Female participants were also more integrationist than males. Indeed, it is quite common for levels of tolerance or integration to ease, or even harden, with more exposure to other cultures. The key point here is that strategies of acculturation are continually reappraised in the light of positive and negative experiences (Bluic et al., 2018).

THE ACCULTURATING TOURIST

Whilst acculturation is often portrayed as a slow, incremental process, it has nevertheless been used to understand tourist behaviour. Holidays are more fleeting travel experiences than migration or study abroad, yet travel for pleasure still involves intercultural encounter, periods of adjustment and adaptation. It has all the requisite conditions for acculturation (Rasmi et al., 2014) albeit in a compressed form. Visitors in tourist destinations must still negotiate new languages, behavioural codes and attitudes. In this context, we can see that some tourists are more likely to integrate into their surroundings than others are.

Mass tourism typically channels travellers towards experiences that are familiar, shielding them from exotica, reflecting an acculturative strategy of separation. There is a tendency to recreate home comforts on-the-go, seeking scant contact with the host culture (Rasmi et al., 2014), perhaps even avoiding it altogether. Consider the gated, all-inclusive holiday resorts which many tourists never leave, unless they are chaperoned by representatives of the tourist industry. These tourists mainly interact with representatives of host cultures who work in hotels, restaurants and attractions. On the other hand, independent tourists typically seek novel experiences, consonant with an acculturation strategy of integration. Beyond the bubble of tourism, we find those who perhaps prefer to be called travellers, rather than tourists, sharing food, habits and customs alongside locals. These travellers would align most with an assimilationist strategy. We may think here of the traveller who aspires to blend in, dressing and acting to avoid identifying themselves with other tourists, studying and speaking the local language where possible, eschewing designated tourist sites/sights and (historically perhaps) hiding their map or guidebook as they walk down the street (Lepp & Gibson, 2003). A fourth acculturation strategy, that of marginalisation, would be illustrated by those who prefer solitary pursuits, away from it (us/them) all (Yiannakis & Gibson, 1992), such as mountaineering or hiking, favouring integration with nature rather than with culture.

In researching tourist acculturation strategies, Rasmi et al. (2014) found integration to be the preferred strategy, which is consistent with general findings about acculturation. Part of the enjoyment of long-term travel can be adapting to a new host culture (Berno & Ward, 2005). More surprisingly, they found marginalisation to be the second most popular strategy ('striving for solitude'). Whilst marginalisation is generally regarded as being maladaptive for long term travel, such as migration, for tourism it carries more positive connotations. For some people, being on holiday is less about fitting in or learning the norms of a new culture (integrating), and more about doing one's own thing, escaping the crowd or communing with nature.

For the tourist industry, acculturation theory can be a handy indicator of traveller needs and motivations. Integrationists would seemingly be inclined to look for adventures which preserve some elements of their own culture, such as familiar food or home comforts, whilst at the same time experimenting with new ways of life. For example, for some devout travellers, a travel experience which facilitates the opportunity to maintain religious practices would be attractive when selecting a travel destination. Meanwhile, a pull factor for assimilationists would be the opportunity for immersion in the host destination. Travel companies and tourist boards would do well to advertise the unique features of destinations here, offering the chance to try something different. They might also use some of the psychological theory outlined here when designing their holiday experiences and advertising campaigns for travellers and tourists with differing strategies in mind.

FLUENT IN TWO CULTURES: BICULTURALISM

We have so far learned that whether we apply acculturation theory to long or short-term travel, one popular strategy for dealing with intercultural encounter is a compromise position, known as integration. Typically, this involves combining a desire to maintain elements of the known (food, language, dress, attitudes), whilst simultaneously sampling elements of the unknown. This integrationist acculturation strategy has acquired a life of its own in psychology, under the guise of biculturalism, defined as

> an umbrella term to refer to any case in which a person endorses at least one heritage culture and at least one receiving culture.
> (Nguyen & Benet-Martínez, 2013: 3)

Bicultural travellers attempt to be fluent in the values and norms of two cultures. A form of adjustment in emotion, behaviour and attitude, it is generally regarded as positive, with desirable outcomes such as cultural flexibility, new behavioural repertoires, a second language and diverse social networks in other countries (Ozer, 2017). Bicultural travellers simultaneously endorse their own cultural heritage and that of another (Schwartz et al., 2016). Some early research associated biculturalism with acculturative stress, isolation and identity confusion (Rudmin, 2003). More recently it has been viewed in a positive light. As more people worldwide are exposed to more cultures, the wholehearted rejecting of one's heritage culture in favour of another (assimilation) is less common (Schwartz et al., 2016).

For example, a person who migrates from one nation to another has the option to simultaneously engage in the language, culture and media of their newfound culture, and with their contacts and culture back home. Arguably, with the availability of social media and digital living, integrationist strategies of adjustment are easier to pursue than ever before (Schwartz et al., 2016). Biculturalism has become mainstream. Research with adolescent migrant populations suggests that as well as being the most common acculturation strategy (Berry, 2017), biculturalism usually yields the most favourable psychological outcomes (Schwartz et al., 2016) such as enhanced openness to people from other cultures (Lee, 2010).

Nguyen & Benet-Martínez (2013) reviewed research into the effects of biculturalism on three other indicators of wellbeing; psychological adjustment (including emotional wellbeing, life satisfaction, positive affect, self-esteem, anxiety, depression, loneliness), sociocultural adjustment (including academic achievement, career success, social skills, delinquency, risk behaviours), and health-related adjustment (including headaches, back pains, physical activity, diet). This was a large-scale study, with 159 separate samples of participants across multiple cultural regions. It supported the view of biculturalism as a positive acculturative strategy. Bicultural individuals were significantly better adjusted than monocultural ones. Correspondingly, individuals who were better adjusted were usually found to be bicultural. Overall, integrationist strategies were associated with better levels of psychological adjustment than were strategies like separation or assimilation. Although this large-scale study over-represented research from particular regions (Latin American and Hispanic samples in the U.S.), it does endorse the view that biculturalism is associated with enhanced psychological wellbeing. It's good to be fluent in two cultures.

AT THE BORDER: THE LIMINAL EXPERIENCE OF ACCULTURATION

There have always been itinerants, drifters, hobos, restless souls.

(Bruder, *Nomadland*, 2021: 2)

At the heart of the experience of acculturation is a disorienting feeling, experienced by anyone in transit, who finds themself between places in a kind of experiential Nomadland. Psychology has often neglected transient humans, focusing instead on people who are either in one place or another (Beckstead, 2010). Even a branch of psychology which specialises in culture, cross-cultural psychology, mostly compares the behaviours of those who reside in two or more cultural locations ('Americans v. Chinese', 'Westerners v. Easterners'), as though they are permanent fixtures there. The concept of acculturation is an attempt to correct this imbalance.

For the acculturating person, the experience of being (metaphorically, at least) at the border between two cultures can be unsettling. Think of the migrant, struggling to make sense of novel bureaucratic processes, or the traveller trying to figure out a transport system, or the international student trying to study Mathematics or Psychology in a second language. This said, the inbetweenness of acculturation has its advantages too. Personal development, multilingualism, adaptation and learning are all consequences of a dynamic process which enables the self to develop in more than one culture. The lure of this hybrid state attracts many people to travel for work, study or leisure (Kwak, 2010).

> If acculturation experiences were only oppressive, stressful, and debilitating, foreign food restaurants and foreign tourism should not exist.
>
> (Rudmin, 2003: 326)

For the migrant, tourist, pilgrim or international student, whether making sense of a new culture is challenging, enlightening or stressful, there is something transformative about it. Travellers are torn between places. Acculturation feels like an experience of simultaneous worlds, casting travellers as outsiders in a new place, whilst similarly reminding them of where they are from. Difference is highlighted at every turn. Newness is felt with heightened lucidity in novel, yet everyday settings (Overhearing novel voices in the street, catching the odour of a new food, seeing products with peculiar names on the supermarket shelves). For most travellers, acculturation feels like moving away from the centre of one's world, towards something, somewhere, somebody new. Conversely, for devout travellers on a sacred pilgrimage, the direction of travel may be away from home but towards something which is at the centre of a belief system, identity or culture (Beckstead, 2010). Either way, the transient, acculturative state is a border crossing, a movement between cultures, towards new experience, away from normal routines. For all travellers, acculturation combines longing for here and for there, bringing with it changes in behaviours, identities, values, and selves (Beckstead, 2010).

This sense of being in-between places, this liminality (Turner & Turner, 1978) can be a motivator for travel in the first place. Travellers are attracted by the uncertainty associated with border crossings. The paradox of acculturation is the desire for something new and the security of holding onto the known. And yet there is another way for us to understand travel as a liminal experience. Besides the tension between participating in two cultures, in the known and the unknown, the transformation of acculturation also takes place at another kind of border. One that delineates our internal world (the mind) and the external world (culture or place). As we travel from the familiar to the new, we construct new meanings, adopt new attitudes, make lasting changes to how we see the world. Our attitudes and beliefs about ourselves, and about the places we visit, change. Because our perceptions and beliefs about the world change, so the world itself changes. These changes themselves take place at a liminal space, between the inner mind and the world outside. We change ourselves and the world as we move through it.

> The liminal, or sense of the extraordinary, is not simply given in the external realm, nor is it to be found isolated in the imagination or attitude of the traveller. Both aspects are necessary, and it is at the boundary of the external (objective) and internal (subjective) worlds that the liminal occurs and also creates the necessary conditions for indescribable feelings of awe, reverence and joy.
>
> (Beckstead, 2010: 392)

TRAVEL BROADENS THE MIND: COSMOPOLITANISM

We have so far explored intercultural encounters that come with travel through the lens of acculturation and biculturalism. To conclude, we will consider the frequently asked question; 'does travel broaden the mind?' using an interdisciplinary concept that psychologists and geographers often deploy when writing about the experience of travel. *Cosmopolitanism* has been defined as

> a state of identity without borders that is accessible to those able to engage in voluntary migration across multiple cultures.
>
> Sobre-Denton (2011: 80)

More of a worldview than a set of attitudes and behaviours, cosmopolitanism is an outlook, a moral perspective, from which humanity appears as a unified, global community, transcending tribal allegiances such as nationality (Bur-Bayram, 2018). Cosmopolitanism reflects a willingness to take risks by embracing otherness. Perhaps travel frees us up to see the world through cosmopolitan eyes, offering a privileged viewpoint and broadening our minds in the process. Cosmopolitan travellers identify with multiple different cultures simultaneously, which are therefore free to coexist in an individual. When encountering new cultures, often but not exclusively through travel, the cosmopolitan is able to

> incorporate the manners, habits, languages and social customs of cities throughout the world.
>
> (Scruton, 2007: 146)

There are obvious parallels with biculturalism here. However, cosmopolitanism emphasises the coexistence in one individual of multiple cultural repertoires (not just two). Cosmopolitan citizens of the world embrace patterns of behaviour and consumption that sample multiple cultures through diverse tastes and experiences. They frequent multi-cultural cities, sampling ideas, dress, food and music from around the world. Their social circle is likely to comprise of representatives from many nations. Not everyone who travels is destined to develop a cosmopolitan outlook. Nevertheless, cosmopolitanism is a consequence of a world in which global travel and communication are increasingly common.

A state of openness to diverse behaviours, lifestyles and traditions (Skey, 2013) sits well with the notion of mind-broadening, educational, enlightening travel. Perhaps travel does broaden the mind. This harks back to the European Grand Tour, which was practised by privileged Europeans between 1600 and 1900. For economic elites the tour followed a well-signposted itinerary of European cities and universities. Until mass tourism came with the railways and steamships of the early 19th century, this excursion was a rite of passage and pre-requisite for participation in fashionable society. The notion of travel as a transformative, enlightening practice, open to those who can afford it, persists today (Delanty, 2006). There remains an association between (at least extended) travel and cosmopolitanism (Amit, 2015). This said, in the 21st century, a cosmopolitan outlook is no longer the reserve of mobile, privileged elites. Broadening the mind through intercultural encounter is an experience which is more widely accessible in an age of global digital communication, mobile workforces and cheap flights. Like acculturation and biculturalism, a cosmopolitan world view is a survival strategy in a time of diversity and globalisation (Datta, 2009). It is a way of navigating the challenge of encountering new places and it has been observed in various populations, including students participating in study abroad programs (Oikonomidoy & Williams, 2013). Being well-versed in the music, food and language of diverse cultures is both an aspiration and a reward for those with open minds and busy travel itineraries.

Like acculturation, cosmopolitanism varies in degree and type between individuals (Szerszynski & Urry, 2002). For example, extended periods of travel lead some to gravitate towards purposive cosmopolitanism, as opposed to so-called xenocentrism (Cleveland & Balakrishnan, 2019). A purposive cosmopolitan reflects an openness to broad cultural diversity, an ability to navigate multiple, diverse cultural environments (restaurants, universities, travel hubs).

Contrastingly, xenocentrics reserve their feelings of allegiance for one particular newly encountered cultural group (more comparable to biculturalism or assimilation, perhaps). In each of these forms of cosmopolitanism, the key characteristic remains an attitude of openness to more than one culture. Far from always being motivated by idealism or a belief in the global community, cosmopolitanism can take a more practical form. So-called banal cosmopolitanism has been identified as more of a survival strategy for frequent travellers; a conscious effort at being flexible in different cultural circumstances, with less of a lasting effect on core identities. As Skey (2013) writes, this amounts to

> a 'strategic' form of cosmopolitanism, in which openness to others is undertaken with instrumental or practical goals rather than a desire to further 'progressive aims or values'.
>
> (2013: 241).

Although the concept of cosmopolitanism can help us understand intercultural encounter, we should be wary of labelling people as 'cosmopolitan', thus ignoring the fluidity of identity and experience (Gillespie et al., 2010). After all, this is not a once and for all category or an exclusive club with a lifelong membership. Some people assume a cosmopolitan outlook for a few months, when opportunities for travel arise. Cosmopolitanism is a globally oriented outlook, to be adopted from time to time, depending on circumstances and surroundings. There is a danger not only in labelling well-travelled, culturally experienced individuals as cosmopolitans, but also as being somehow 'more rounded' than those who lack the opportunity to mix with outgroups (Gillespie et al., 2010). Not everyone has access to intercultural encounter, travel or cultural diversity.

The aim of this chapter has been to unpack the experience of intercultural encounter at a time when it is increasingly common, though far from universal. Movement between borders of nation and culture, short or long-term, can be transformative, sometimes stressful, sometimes mind-broadening. For travellers of various types, intercultural encounter requires adaptations in behaviours, feelings and attitudes that change the way we view the places around us, and the way we view ourselves. The emergence in psychology of the acculturated, bicultural and cosmopolitan traveller reminds us that we owe many aspects of our identity to our interactions with diverse people and places.

8

DETOUR: PSYCHOGEOGRAPHY
AND THE ART OF SLOW TRAVEL

DRIFTING AMBULANCE

For some travellers, journeying is just as important as arriving and routes are just as important as destinations (Spinney, 2009). There is even a loosely constructed group of artists, psychologists, geographers and philosophers who love travel but barely care for destinations at all. This detour in our journey through the psychology of travel focuses on the work of this group, who are known as psychogeographers. They offer a unique perspective on our relationship with the places we move through. Psychogeography celebrates slow, meandering travel, usually on foot, more than it celebrates getting from A to B. Whilst it sounds like a straightforward hybrid of psychology and geography, it is really a homeless, multidisciplinary field straddling art, literature, geography and social science. It is a critical stance on how we design, inhabit and report on familiar and unfamiliar places. Psychogeography is an umbrella under which artists, philosophers, psychologists, geographers and literary figures have congregated to discuss varieties of travel experience since the mid-20th century. One of its founding figures, French critical theorist Guy Debord, determined that the primary aim of psychogeography should be

DOI: 10.4324/9781003215530-8

> The study of the precise law and specific effects of the geographical environment, consciously organized or not, on the emotions and behavior of individuals.
>
> (Debord, 1955: 12)

Psychogeography found its feet in Paris in the 1950s under the tutelage of a group of intellectuals and activists known as the Situationist International (Coverley, 2006; Morley, 2021). Lamenting the modernisation and gentrification of Paris, this group challenged what they saw as an abhorrent, corporate transformation of their beloved city. They developed their own defiant method to get themselves heard. Based on meandering, writing and critical reportage, they developed a walking method known as the *dérive* ('drift' in English), which has been defined as

> An unorganized and aimless, yet significant, walk.
>
> (Antony & Henry, 2005: 21)

The Situationist International explored our relations with place through poetry, pranks and purposive drifting. Since it first emerged on the boulevards of Paris, psychogeography has been adopted and adapted by contemporary researchers and activists across several fields, including some on the outskirts of psychology. It retains a critical stance on travel and urban design and continues to express itself through small mobile acts that combine drifting, walking, observing, reporting and provoking a reaction through research, art and reportage.

As well as being synonymous with the dérive, psychogeography was, especially in its early days, personified as the figure of the *flâneur*; a sauntering, historically almost always male, drifting observer of street level society (Coverley, 2006). A hipster of the boulevards who walked and wrote. Strolling with no particular destination in mind, the flâneur traced paths around urban spaces, using slow travel as a medium for composing critical musings about how we relate to our surroundings. This idle traveller values playful, provocative exploration and reportage more than getting anywhere in particular. Whilst most travellers fear getting lost, a flâneur revels in disorientation.

TRAVEL DISRUPTION

Ambulation: moving from place to place
Perambulation: traveling through, about, around, up and down

Chambers 21st Century Dictionary

Psychogeographers perambulate more than they ambulate. Just as the Situationist International challenged the utilitarian, commercially motivated modernisation of Paris, psychogeography challenges commercially driven, habitual ways of designing, perceiving and apprehending places (Bridger, 2010). For the flâneur, walking is an exploratory, defiant, non-conformist act; a deliberately exploratory and disorientating form of pedestrian punk psychology. The irreverent influence of psychogeography on countercultural movements such as critical theory, contemporary art and punk rock is widely acknowledged (Antony & Henry, 2005; Morley, 2021). Artists and researchers who do psychogeography travel through cities, usually on foot, observing chance encounters, questioning dominant ways of seeing the world, revealing marvels buried in the everyday (Pinder, 2005: 404), often taking photographs or diarising. Using routine perambulation to explore places, psychogeographers deploy diverse media (art, poetry, photography, prose, video, sound) to explore how we experience and attach meanings to our surroundings through daily, often repetitive, travel routines. The walking method, popularized by the lone Parisian flâneur, thrives on everyday observation (de Certeau, 1984), quotidian experience, challenging received wisdom about what counts as travel, what counts as a destination, what counts as a journey, what counts as a holiday.

German philosopher Walter Benjamin was perhaps the original Parisian flâneur. He settled in Paris in the 1920s and taught himself the art of straying. For his book *One-Way Street* (Benjamin, 2009) and his (unfinished) *Arcades Project* (Benjamin, 2009) he explored a labyrinth of ornate, glass-roofed, pedestrianised arcades, theorising them as symbols of the journey Paris was making towards becoming a commercially driven, consumerist city (Solnit, 2014). Benjamin was a detached man of leisure whose natural environment was the disruptive arcades. These fluid spaces were simultaneously inside and outside. It was permissible to walk there, though less acceptable to do so without purpose, whilst resisting the commercial appeal of consumerism. Walking, but not buying, the flâneur challenges the commercial aspirations of individual vendors and of capitalism at large. As if to highlight his preference for proceeding at a leisurely pace, at odds with the accelerating economy, Benjamin mimicked the popular Parisian habit of walking with pet turtles, a practice which was (slowly) gaining popularity in the 1840s (Solnit, 2014).

Figure 8.1 For his unfinished *Arcades Project* Walter Benjamin explored a labyrinth of ornate, glass-roofed, pedestrianised arcades

Early theorists of walking, like Benjamin and Debord, urged us to travel and encounter new places whilst eschewing commodifying aspects of tourism. They promoted the practice of urban drift whilst disrupting conventional, utilitarian motives for travel (work, tourism, commerce). Psychogeographers are motivated by travel modes which valorise mundane discoveries, unplanned encounters and unconventional uses of space. Two separate London-based walking projects epitomise the dissenting spirit of psychogeography. In London Orbital (2002) Iain Sinclair walked 120 miles around the M25 motorway which encircles the English capital, poetically reporting the commercial sprawl, growth and decay of its urban and rural edge-lands. In his essay Walking to New York (2007), English novelist Will Self challenged the demarcation of pedestrian space and the corporate restrictions it imposes on urban walking. To bookend a flight from London to New York Self mischievously walked from his home to London's Heathrow Airport (26 miles), then from New York's JFK Airport into Manhattan (20 miles). The spaces he encountered are not designed for walking. His perilous journey led him down expressways, which, whilst reserved for motorised traffic, afforded detailed observation of spaces that usually go unnoticed by those who only view the world through a windscreen. Using walking as a peaceable protest and humorous reportage Self captures the spirit of psychogeography by dwelling on a dissenting journey, rather than on his destination

> I reached the road tunnel that plunges beneath the runways and into the terminal complex, only to find the following sign 'No pedestrian access. Go Back to the Renaissance'. This was, of course, a hotel from which you are required to take a shuttle bus.
>
> (Self, 2007: 15)

Another popular illustration of psychogeography-inspired anti-tourism is the wonderfully entertaining Lonely Planet Guide to Experimental Travel (Antony & Henry, 2005). This guidebook with a difference (even more disorientating coming from a publisher normally associated with conventional travel guides) presents playful suggestions of psychogeographical pranks to celebrate disruption and drift in the city of your choice. Try these on your next city break;

Backpacking at home: Travel to your nearest airport, then take a bus back into your city and head for the local backpacker hostel. Spend a few days meeting fellow travelers and enjoy the sights and sounds of your own city, taking photographs and living on a shoestring.

Alternating travel: Defamiliarise yourself from your own city and discover it anew. Take a walk during which you take the first right turn, then the first left turn, then the next right, and so on forth, until something blocks your path. Start again.

Counter-tourism: Use a conventional guidebook unconventionally to gain an alternative perspective of a city. Visit recommended attractions, turn your back and take a photograph. Alternatively, use the book to guide you to local attractions, but always take the opposite turn to the one recommended. What do you discover?

Slow return travel: Visit a far-off destination using the quickest, most direct route possible. Make your return journey slowly, incrementally, using a combination of ambulation and local public transportation. How do the experiences differ?

Bureaucratic odyssey: Whilst visiting a city of your choice, base your travel itinerary on availing yourself of places of administrative, rather than touristic or historic, importance, in order to see the place through the eyes of those who live there. Spend time in waiting rooms, doing photocopying, making medical appointments and seeking routine repairs.

Aesthetic travel: When visiting local attractions in your chosen city, rather than just taking photographs, experiment with other art forms to record your experiences. Write a poem about a police station. Paint a picture of a roundabout. Make a sound recording in a bakery.

WALKS OF ART

As we travel through places our perceptions of them change. Just as people affect places, places affect us as we move through them. Whether we are talking about thousands of people visiting a place just once, or one person crossing a field hundreds of times, the effect cuts both ways. People and places are mutually constitutive.

> I began walking my own city's streets as a teenager and walked them so long that both they and I changed.
>
> (Solnit, 2014: 194)

The mundane, sometimes repetitive journeys that punctuate our daily lives are routine rituals that allow us to walk, ride or pedal ourselves into meaningful places. These rituals leave their mark on us and on the landscape. One thinks here of unofficial paths worn across carpets, meadows and quadrangles.

Figure 8.2 The repetitive journeys that punctuate our daily lives leave their mark on us and on the landscape

Several artists and researchers have used creative, mobile methods to explore interactions between people and landscapes. For example, in projects using photovoice, participants make photographs of familiar journeys and are then invited to reflect on them in interviews (Budig et al., 2018). Similarly, go-along or walking interviews (Moles, 2007; Stevenson & Ordu, 2016) are an excellent method for exploring peoples' relationships with familiar routes and spaces. In a third mobile method, known as soundwalking, participants make sound recordings along familiar journeys and are then interviewed about the way in which sonic environments affect their relationships with place (Traux, 1978). Creative methods such as these have all produced walking-based artworks and research outputs that have echoes of psychogeography. The handful of projects reviewed here demonstrate how psychogeography has inspired artists and researchers to understand the often personal, idiosyncratic nature of travel and mobility, albeit usually on a small scale.

In *Line Made by Walking* (1967), English artist Richard Long created a temporary artwork to illustrate the marks travellers (tourists or commuters) leave on the landscape. His line in the grass, etched out across a meadow from his own repetitive walking, destined to fade or become overgrown, can be read as a critique of consumerism, a statement about the temporariness of artworks bought and sold at inflated prices, or a comment about the lines we leave behind us as we travel across the land. Blurring the boundary between sculpture and photography, ultimately it would be Long's photograph of the line (not the line itself) that would later be displayed, bought and sold.

In a collection entitled *Lunch Poems* (1964), American poet Frank O'Hara used his daily midday walks to explore and document the blurred relationship between himself and the New York streets. *Lunch Walks* simultaneously tells us something about the streets and the author, who writes as though to a strolling companion (Solnit, 2014). Using breaks from his job at the Museum of Modern Art, O'Hara deployed walking as a daily routine for organising his thoughts and celebrating the prosaic. A solitary poet, observing and reporting the streets in bite-size verses, O'Hara wrote about themes of loneliness and anonymity from street level. There are clear parallels between Parisian flâneur and New York poet.

In a mischievous walking-based project, *Venetian Suite* (1998), French artist Sophie Calle engaged with themes of surveillance whilst projecting her thoughts onto a man she met at a party (known enigmatically as Henri B, who unwittingly became a participant in her experiment). After becoming acquainted with him in Paris, she surreptitiously followed him as he relocated to Venice, then spent subsequent months shadowing his movements and exploring the city on foot. Playing interpersonally with ideas that are usually practised at a governmental or institutional level (detection, suspicion, surveillance), Calle documented Venice through movements initiated by Henri B. In the spirit of psychogeography, *Venetian Suite* guides us through the city with neither author nor reader knowing where we are going. The resulting book and sequence of photographs is a travel dossier which documents Calle's pursuit as she contacts hotels, visits a police station, and even persuades one resident to let her photograph Henri from her window. What struck Calle as most interesting about the curious style of travel she adopted for *Venetian Suite* was how it led her to investigate a place through someone else's intentions, in an escapade which combines elements of international espionage, cold war crime thriller and a package holiday, where every travel decision is out of your hands.

In the field of cultural geography several researchers have created walking-based projects to illustrate the role of the senses in our experience of visiting new places. True to the critical tradition of psychogeography, many of these researchers reject purely observational research, instead experimenting with how we apprehend the world through sound, smell and taste. Designed for "investigating people's relationship with soundscapes and the built environment" (Adams & Bruce, 2008: 6), soundwalking is a tactic for studying how people get to know places they visit by listening and generating knowledge which is specifically based on sound. One geographer asked participants to walk familiar routes and make a sonic portrait of a place by mixing interview fragments and field recordings, producing a soundscape

composition of a Scottish landscape (Gallagher, 2015). This partici-
pant-led model combines the influence of the dérive with the variation
that the resulting recording features multiple voices, rather than that of
the solitary flâneur. Another example of sound-based walking research
is the commented walk model. This is a walking interview where
the researcher accompanies a participant on a route with the latter
describing and recording the landscape. Similarly, in the shadow-walk
method (Corringham, 2008), after being guided along meaningful
routes by a participant, the researcher re-walks the routes alone and
develops remixed recordings or performances of place. These sound-
based works are valuable for those who want to design inclusive travel
destinations, and who need to understand the experiences of travellers
who rely on sonic aspects of environment for their satisfaction. After
all, the travel experience amounts to far more than mere spectacle.

Olfaction has also been used to explore travel experiences. Impressions of new locations, as well as memories of previously visited
places, are often powerfully conveyed through taste and smell. To find
out how newly arrived migrants develop meaningful attachments to
a new city through the senses, one case study used taste and smell
alongside psychogeographical walking methods (Stevenson & Ordu,
2016). During on-the-go interviews in her newly adopted city (Manchester, England), A, a migrant from Tunisia, recounted stories of her
former home city (Tunis) whilst visiting a handful of Mancunian sites
that evoked North African memories. She led the interviewer through
aromatic sites that seemed to her to join Manchester and Tunis by
virtue of connecting tastes and smells. A fruit market, a covered pave-
ment café connecting two streets ('A place between two places'), a dough-
nut shop and a retro clothes emporium, were all meaningful sites
along an evocative walking route that transported the senses. Mancunian smells and tastes recalled memories of Tunis. The imagined,
hyphenated city of 'Man-Tunis' was later commemorated in a series
of playful picture postcards combining photographs from the walk
with A's descriptions of comparable Tunisian locations. The hybrid
postcards, a creative response to a migrant's relocation from one
city to another, deliberately confuse memories and conflate stories.

Manchester and Tunis coexist in pictures, words and multisensory (olfactory, gustatory) evocations from sites along a walking journey. In this example A explains the link between a Tunisian medina (old town) and a Mancunian retro clothes emporium, united by smell;

> They sell lots of leather bags here. And there's a specific shop in the medina that this reminds me of. There's a guy who sells camel leather, like camel leather bags. And there's that musty smell of old, cured leather and you smell that when you walk down these stairs, and it just sort of takes you back in time.
>
> (Stevenson & Ordu, 2016: 182)

Figure 8.3 A retro clothes emporium on an evocative walking route that transports the senses

It seems fitting to end this short review of notable psychogeo-graphical projects exploring travel with an enigmatic, Mexican-based work by Belgian artist Francis Alÿs. In *Sometimes Making Something Leads to Nothing* (Alÿs & Ferguson, 2019), Alÿs produced a short film of himself effortfully (at first at least) pushing a huge block of ice (the size of a small wardrobe) around the streets of Mexico City for nine hours, until it became small enough to be kicked along the sidewalk. The video features sights, sounds and storefronts of the city, document-ing its daily working and walking routines. Watching the film, you empathise with the efforts of the artist as he hefts his melting burden through the heat. Pushing the ice can be read as a symbol of the daily labours of the city's residents, often yielding diminishing rewards. More optimistically, it shows that all you need in order to see the city in a new and unique way is to experience it through the labours of another person, and to set off on a journey whose duration and des-tination are both unclear.

FLÂNEUSE

Psychogeography has often been personified by a lone, usually male wanderer who narrated the city from a leisured perspective (Bassett, 2004). A disproportionately male perspective arguably gave psychoge-ography a bit of a laddish feel, conveying the thrill of walking as though it were an attempt at conquering the city (Rose, 2015; Massey, 2005). Critics see early psychogeography as an exercise in exploring urban travel through the male gaze, with the flâneur portraying the city as

> something feminine, passively there for the taking, a wilder-ness-like space of adventure to be conquered or possessed.
>
> (Bassett, 2004: 403)

Such gendered trends in psychogeography reflect broader attitudes towards walking. Historically, women and men have seldom walked on an equal footing. In 19th-century London females walking alone connoted deviance and prostitution. Lone females were frequently rounded up by the British government, subjected to medical examinations and incarcerated (Solnit, 2014). Everyday language betrays gender discrimination in relation to walking. 'Streetwalker' and 'woman of the street' are feminized phrases with negative associations that are absent in a construction like 'man about town' or 'man in the street'. London in the 1850s had more brothels than schools and charities put together (Solnit, 2014). Across the English Channel, in the 1870s French police criminalised walking women, requiring them to be licensed as prostitutes, restricting them to walking at certain hours of the day. Whilst the flâneur was celebrated in literary circles, opportunities to practice a female dérive were severely limited. Arguably, the female urban traveller has never been fully considered a flâneur since she has lacked the independence and sense of detachment that the role demands (Solnit, 2014). Even now, opportunities to wander 'aimlessly, yet purposefully' are more limited for female travellers visiting unfamiliar places.

But things have changed. Contemporary psychogeography increasingly explores urban travel experience from a female perspective (Bassett, 2004; Rose, 2015). There is a shift towards reworking the concept of the flâneur, rather than simply shoehorning women's experiences of walking into a masculine mould (Elkin, 2016). In her book *Flâneuse: Women Walk the City*, (2016) American, Paris-based author Lauren Elkin presents the case for the distinctive, transformational female walking experience. After moving to Paris, Elkin described the freedom she found in habitual walking and in always being on the lookout for the accidental and unexpected. During stints in New York, London, Venice and Tokyo, she retraces stories of notable female walking artists and writers, including Sophie Calle and Virginia Woolf. She writes of cities as spaces of possibility which move through and around her as she walks, sustaining life all the while. For Elkin's flâneuse, walking affords a state of inbetweenness, through which places and selves are continually being discovered, constructed and renewed.

Another notable, inspiring homage to female walking comes from Lizzy Stewart's *Walking Distance* (2022), a graphic essay about the experience of being a woman walking in London. Merging image and text, the book is both observational and contemplative. Stewart examines her life and reflects on what her family, friends and society expect of her. Using walking, drawing and writing, Stewart shares her moment-to-moment experiences alongside reflections on her parallel life journey. She ruminates on her self-portraits whilst walking us through her lifecycle, often from the viewpoint of other people walking in the street

> Sometimes I take a step that splits me in two, into the woman who is walking and another woman who steps back, to watch. I wonder what I look like, do I look like an adult with an adult life?
>
> (2022: 5)

Walking Distance offers a personal meditation on walking, using beautifully crafted images that reflect the anonymity, connectedness and security of street-level travel ('*walking in London is when I feel most certain*'). Walking is used here to reflect on, rather than critique, the design of the city, showing how we can explore our own identities through perambulation. Walking can teach us that actively, routinely familiarising yourself with your environment is a way to learn about yourself.

If *Walking Distance* explores the city through the experiences of the lone flâneuse, elsewhere feminist psychogeography has also experimented with more collaborative forms of walking. Acknowledging the historical lack of inclusivity of the term flâneuse, Morag Rose (2015) seeks to widen the appeal of psychogeography to become more gender and disability inclusive. One manifestation of this change is to democratise the dérive as a community-based practice. Rose pitches psychogeography to anyone and everyone, not just academics and artists. An activist in a community called the Loiterers Resistance Movement she uses shared urban walks to prompt conversations amongst equals, with no established or sole leader, in order to explore the communal experience of urban space. True to the spirit of psychogeography, these regular group dérives are inspired by the rejection of the utilitarian idea that travel is about moving from A to B. Instead, routes are created by arbitrary rules (throwing dice, following directions indicated by CCTV cameras, visiting statues that commemorate famous women). Participants are encouraged to get involved in designing walking routes, thus diluting reliance on expert guides. Group dérives are a departure from early, solitary psychogeography. They value shared experience, democratise decision-making and provide a safer experience for those who are reluctant to walk alone. The empowering ethos of the Loiterer's Resistance Movement transforms space into something shared and aims to build a tapestry of stories with multiple voices. This resonates with an increasingly popular practice for travellers and tourists, the themed urban walk (guided or otherwise). Guided walks offer an environmentally sustainable form or educational slow travel that is ideal for getting to know people and places. After all, not every traveller wants to wander the streets alone.

Psychogeography is an alternative travel practice which encourages dissent. Its playful strategies are underpinned by critical ideas about how and where we travel. Psychogeography disproportionately concerns itself with slow, urban travel, with many of its more celebrated contributors focusing on the cities of Paris and London. Despite this narrow focus it has contributed to several fields and disciplines, across the arts and academia. In psychology is has inspired a number of innovative qualitative mobile research methods, such as on-the-go interviewing and soundwalking. An interdisciplinary approach which willfully occupies the outskirts of mainstream psychology, psychogeography continues to challenge conventions about the nature of travel, and to yield a range of creative and critical work

9

WHERE DO WE GO FROM HERE?: TRAVEL IN AN AGE OF ECO-ANXIETY

TRAVEL INTERRUPTION

However strong the desire to travel, global events can sometimes get in the way. A recession, a pandemic, the climate emergency, can all lead to travel interruptions. The COVID-19 lockdown left many frequent flyers feeling grounded and socially isolated, their subjective wellbeing taking a nosedive (De Vos, 2020). Economic, climate and health crises remind us that travelling, especially internationally, is subject to the vicissitudes of global events and cannot be taken for granted.

Before 2019 travel and tourism were amongst the fastest growing sectors in the global economy. Whatever the motive for travel, the underlying trend had been upward for decades. International arrivals soared from 25 million to 1.186 billion between 1950 and 2015 (UNWTO, 2022). This upward trajectory has been interrupted from time to time, notably by the 2003 SARS (severe acute respiratory syndrome) epidemic (affecting China, Hong Kong, Taiwan, Singapore and Canada), and by the 2009 global financial crisis (Glaesser et al., 2017). COVID-19 interrupted international travel to the extent that it restricted most people to exploring their own neighbourhoods in 2020, whilst airports and railway stations stood empty. By 2021 a recovery was underway, with a 27% rise in nights spent in EU tourist accommodation (Masterson, 2022) compared with 2020 (still 37 %

DOI: 10.4324/9781003215530-9

less than before 2019). Whilst the desire to travel seems insatiable, recoveries are unequally distributed. In 2021, Spain, Greece and Croatia welcomed 70% more visitors than in the previous year, meanwhile Austria, Latvia and Slovakia saw an 18% shortfall (Masterson, 2022).

Global events that interrupt travel are varied and numerous, obliging travellers and providers to adapt and roll with the times. In the future, travel will undoubtedly continue to be popular, though it will surely be subject to future crises.

TRAVEL IN UNCERTAIN TIMES

Even during stable times travel can provoke fear (of something specific, like flying) and anxiety (a more generalized unease) (see *Chapter 4*). Fear and anxiety are often associated with new experiences, so there is little wonder that travel evokes both. As if to exacerbate the effect, going somewhere new during a pandemic, war or climate emergency, can be yet more challenging. For example, taking a holiday after the spike of a global health scare can provoke feelings of trepidation despite (or perhaps because of) the relaxation of quarantine and social distancing rules. Equally, not travelling can make us feel frustrated and inhibited. For regular travellers, long periods of staying at home and avoiding contact with other people are associated with heightened anxiety. Lengthy periods of lockdown can also increase fear of travel in the future (Zheng et al., 2019).

History suggests that getting reinfected with the travel bug after an enforced period of abstinence can take time. After the 2003 SARS outbreak, fear of infection saw a prolonged collapse in outward travel from East Asia, with demand falling from 702.6 million in 2002 to 694 million in 2003 (World Tourism Organization, 2011). SARS had a lasting impact on Chinese domestic tourists too, with journeys decreasing and fear levels rising, along with the perception of risk related to travel (Wen et al., 2005). In the wake of both SARS and the 2009 H1N1 (swine flu) outbreaks, many travellers met epidemiological risks with behaviour change, often becoming more cautious in their choices (Shamshiripour et al., 2020). Three years after the Ebola outbreak in Sierra Leone, international arrivals to West Africa were still running at half those of pre-epidemic levels (World Travel & Tourism Council, 2018). Additionally, in the era of COVID-19 and accelerating global warming, many people are opting out of long-distance air travel, either for environmental reasons or for fear of being infected (Shamshiripour et al., 2020). In one study, residents of Chicago were asked if they expected their flying habits to change in the future; 43% said yes. Dutch flyers echoed this sentiment (de Haas et al., 2020). The most popular reported reasons for these reductions include safety fears (48%), especially sharing space with others.

Nevertheless, travel habits are unlikely to go into terminal decline. The return to travel following global health crises and economic slumps is typically swift, albeit with adaptations in norms and behaviours. Modifying travel habits in uncertain times involves changing thoughts and behaviours, becoming more cautious, rather than staying at home altogether. The likelihood is that we will get into the travel habit of assessing the threat level posed by each journey, and then estimate our ability to cope ('How risky is this trip and can I overcome the risks?') (Floyd et al., 2000). This calculation involves evaluating our levels of resilience before deciding whether we have the psychological and social resources to overcome potential dangers ('Do I feel like I can spend eight hours in a cabin with people I don't know?', 'Can I rely on the airline to enforce hygiene and social distancing rules?', 'Can I trust my travel companions to act responsibly?')

These decisions differ for different people, destinations, times and activities. It is estimated that those who are extra cautious, or who have higher levels of travel fear, typically resume travel around 4–6 months after travel restrictions are lifted following a major global health scare. Meanwhile those with low travel fear wait for around 1–3 months (Zheng et al., 2021). Rather than avoiding travel altogether, it seems that travellers will go cautiously at first, at least until the world is perceived to be a safer place to visit. A decision to resume travel requires a stock-take of psychological resources and networks of support ('travel companions and providers) that can help us overcome persistent fears and anxieties. After a travel moratorium, there may be a tendency to opt for more local travel options (see Chapter 8), with groups of people we know well (see Chapter 3), in our own bubbles, under our own steam, or with travel companies whom we trust to get us there safely. In other words, traveling in uncertain times is likely to be cautious at first, with a greater prioritizing of self-protection (Chen & Yang, 2019), rather than a selection of destinations based on their beauty or potential for hedonistic escapism (see Chapter 5).

To develop coping strategies and adapt travel norms, we look to travel providers for guidance. For example, we might require them to implement measures relating to hygiene, accessibility and social distancing. To build confidence amongst travellers it has been suggested that travel company communication styles are most effective when they are framed positively ('*please respect the personal space of your fellow travelers to ensure a more comfortable journey*') rather than negatively ('*passengers found encroaching on other passenger's personal space will be seated elsewhere or removed at the next opportunity*') (Zheng et al., 2019). Travel providers have a central role in rebuilding levels of trust in the journey, so that demand for travel will return and anxiety levels fall (Quintal, 2021). Trust in this context is defined as 'reliance on another person or agency under a condition of risk' (Currall & Judge, 1995: 151). It is especially important when travelling, which usually involves multiple people spending prolonged periods in confined spaces, like waiting rooms, aircraft cabins and cruise ships. Indeed, the latter have been labelled as 'floating petri dishes' as they are particularly susceptible to disease transmission (Tan, 2020). Historically, cruises have seen outbreaks of swine flu and COVID-19 (Neuburger & Egger, 2020). In order to encourage passengers to regain confidence in travelling in crowded public spaces after a global health scare, the onus is on the travel industry and regulators to provide sincere guidance (Punyatoya, 2019) and positive messaging to reassure travellers that they will be helped to protect themselves. The confidence to return to travel depends on a partnership between travellers and providers.

DIGITAL NOMADISM

Travel for work has seen considerable adaptations in norms and behaviour in recent times. For many people, the experience of going to work has undergone a spatial revolution. More and more employees have found ways of working without travelling. Digital technologies enable some industries to alter their work-based travel practices and blur the boundaries between home, work and leisure. Welcome to the fluid world of the digital nomad (Hermann & Morris Paris, 2020). Digital nomadism is a smart response to the challenges of working in changing times, where social distancing, work-life balance and sustainable working are increasingly valued. For those wishing to avoid the daily commute, crowded trains, stuffy offices and long-haul flights, digital nomadism offers a solution. Commuting can be superseded by location-independent working, typified by teleconferencing and working from flexible spaces ('*Yes, I'm on the beach but I can still meet my colleagues who are back in the office – or on another beach*'). Digital nomads work almost anywhere, anytime, thanks to the flexible digital infrastructure (Blatt & Gallagher, 2013). Ironically, location independent working brings with it personal freedoms that are often associated with travel, adventure, and escape (Reichenberger, 2018). Unhitching oneself from the office desk opens the door to flexible working, perhaps from home, perhaps from somewhere even more desirable. Drop into a meeting from Phuket, Bali or Venice Beach? No problem. If traditional nomads travel because of work, digital nomads travel whilst working, making their workspace work for them. This lifestyle has the potential to free up time and 'de place' work, as employment is divorced from specific buildings. Digital nomads highlight the contemporary trend towards being on the move, also typified by the rise of the gig economy (Sutherland & Jarrahi, 2017).

Of course, not everyone can be a digital nomad. Many professions (insert your own examples here) require face to face contact. The beach-bound laptop worker with apparent independence may also miss the predictable routine of a stable group of colleagues with a familiar workplace to meet and socialise in. It may also be more difficult for digital nomads to compartmentalise work and life ('I *like to walk away from the office and forget about work until tomorrow*'). To overcome these challenges, some employees have been known to set up ring-fenced, quasi-workspaces in exotic or transient locations, even establishing all-inclusive communities of co-living workspaces (von Zumbusch & Lalicic, 2020). Pop-up, rentable office spaces are increasingly common in towns and cities. These shared, hybrid workplaces are handy places to retreat to when there are jobs to be done when you are on the move. These nomad bubbles are reminiscent of the backpacker internet cafés of the 1990s and 2000s. Although digital nomadism is a lifestyle that only works for some occupations, it can offer a smart way of reducing unnecessary travel, combining work with mobility, avoiding the daily commute and virtually being in two places at once.

UNDERSTANDABLE ECO-ANXIETY

Some global travel interruptions come in waves. They have beginnings, middles and ends. For example, a pandemic has peaks, troughs and periods of respite. Contrastingly, the global climate emergency is almost certainly here to stay. The numbers on climate change are galling. The decade between 2010 and 2020 was one of exceptional global heat, with retreating ice and rising sea levels driven by greenhouse gases. This process is now commonly acknowledged to be the result of human activity (UN Environment Programme, 2021). Average annual temperatures in this decade were the highest on record, with 2019 the second hottest year to date (UN Environment Programme, 2021). Thirty per cent of the world population experience heatwaves on more than 20 days each year, and there is every indication that failing governmental commitments to reduce pollution will push emissions still higher in the decade to come. All this considered, it seems perfectly reasonable to be anxious about the climate emergency (Mkono, 2019). Climate activist Greta Thunberg speaks openly about her own climate change anxiety (Thunberg et al., 2020). She has repeatedly called out inadequate governmental responses to global warming. These concerns reflect a phenomenon known as eco-anxiety, a psychological response to an ongoing climate crisis about which a growing number of people are, with justification, worrying themselves sick.

Eco-anxiety can be felt at various levels along a continuum, ranging from mild to severe. Those who feel it to a medium, significant or severe level are most likely to reevaluate their travel choices (Hickman, 2020). Almost 70% of U.S. citizens reportedly worry about global warming, with around half believing that it will harm them personally (Baudon & Jachens, 2021). Despite the then Australian Prime Minister Scott Morrison telling students who were striking over climate change to be 'less activist', 80% of Australians reportedly feel somewhat or very anxious about climate change on a weekly basis. Eco-anxiety reveals a link between climate change and psychological wellbeing (Pikhala, 2019). It is experienced as a mixture of attitudes and emotions and shows a heightened awareness of the plight of the planet (Pikhala, 2019). At an individual level these attitudes and emotions include fear, anger and powerlessness (Baudon & Jachens, 2021). This generalised sense of anxiety about the future (which could equally be seen as a fear of something specific: environmental collapse) is well-founded on climate science. Hence, it is important for psychologists to avoid pathologising eco-anxiety as a 'psychological condition' (Hickman, 2020).

It is possible to experience eco-anxiety individually, in silence, without a platform or opportunity to share environmental concerns. For the sake of our wellbeing, it is probably better to talk about it. Like all attitudes and emotions, eco-anxiety is socially constructed (Tronello & Gaborieau, 2018). How we feel about the future depends on what we read, observe and hear from our peers. Attitudes, emotions and anxieties are part of a global conversation. Hence, worrying in silence can make us feel more helpless and isolated, resulting in a socially constructed, anxiety-perpetuating, omerta. Arguably, eco-anxiety could be reduced by discussing it or translating it into action. Such conversations have the potential to make us feel less isolated. More importantly, they could increase the likelihood of behavioural change in relation to how we travel in the future.

WHERE DO WE GO FROM HERE?

Environmentally sustainable changes to travel habits can potentially help to reduce eco-anxiety (Büchs et al., 2015), as well as reduce our carbon footprint. From a social psychological perspective (see Chapter 3), changes we make at an individual level ('I want to stop using my car so much') are inevitably made in a social context, often in response to other people's actions ('A friend of mine has started car sharing, which I might try too'). Hence, anyone with a moderate level of climate anxiety might affect other peoples' habits by exerting social influence. Voicing concerns through the mass media, social media, in family conversations, social networks or workplaces, can raise awareness and influence cultural travel norms incrementally.

An example of the mass media being used to affect public opinion about climate change is Davis Guggenheim' documentary An Inconvenient Truth (2006), featuring former U.S. Vice President Al Gore's attempting to educate people about global warming. Reportedly, 69% of people who saw the film said it changed their mind about global warming, 89% said it raised their awareness, and 75% reported a change in habits, including those relating to travel (Fraser, 2019). An example of interpersonal communication being used to change travel behaviour comes from Sweden, where the practice of flygskam (flight shaming), first coined in 2018, called out the contribution of flying to global warming (Mkono, 2019). Flight-shaming seeks to raise awareness and influence others' actions whilst naming, shaming – perhaps even alienating – frequent flyers. Flight-shamers stop flying and often use social media to spark debates about climate change, hoping others will follow suit. They seek to alter attitudes toward travel by exploiting the attitude-behaviour gap, urging those with established environmentally progressive attitudes to change their behavior accordingly, despite the convenience and affordability of flying (Marin-Pantelescu et al., 2019). Such changes would potentially reduce feelings of cognitive dissonance (see Chapter 3) and levels of anxiety amongst travelers with environmentally friendly views and an intention to travel more sustainably. On the downside, the risk of flight-shaming is that it can be confrontational, lacking the power to reach out to those who are not so eco-anxious.

A more conciliatory way of influencing people to reduce their carbon footprint is to supportively encourage anyone already experiencing eco-anxiety to modify their lifestyles (Baudon & Jachens, 2021). This involves connecting with peoples' existing ideas about sustainability, then working with them to formulate lifestyle changes. Reportedly, changing travel habits can ease feelings of eco-anxiety and increase optimism about the future, and make a practical stand against global warming (Baudon & Jachens, 2021). By connecting with like-minded people, the aim of this conciliatory approach is to move away from individualism, towards seeing ourselves as being intrinsically connected to other people and to the natural world (Baudon & Jachens, 2021). One psychological factor which is relevant to making sustainable transport choices is the degree to which we construe ourselves as individuals, or as part of a collective (Pronello & Gaborieau, 2018). Changing travel habits, for example reducing flying frequency or car sharing, reflects a change of self-construal, with a move towards highlighting the inseparability of people from each other, and from the natural world ('*I am part of the environment where I live, and my life choices affect other people and the planet*'). Psychological health services arguably have a role in this process, using interventions such as eco therapy, wherein clients identify natural spaces to visit for therapeutic reasons and work to build a nurturing relationship with it to address eco-anxiety (Panu, 2020).

One case study sought to address eco-anxiety by highlighting feelings of interconnectedness between clients and environments. Carbon Conversations (Büchs et al., 2015) were set up between groups of participants who had experienced eco-anxiety. The aim was to address emotions about climate change and to develop practical responses for reducing anxiety and increasing sustainable travel. Negative emotions about climate change are associated with anxiety, helplessness and disempowerment, which can hamper practical changes in travel habits, leaving people feeling helpless (Panu, 2020). To overcome this, focus groups of 6–8 participants met regularly over several weeks to discuss environmental themes such as energy use and transport choices. These conversations urged participants to engage more positively with their emotions and share their feelings and experiences with others, with a view to creating environmentally conscious lifestyle changes. The focus was on responding to others' emotions and generating ways of living environmentally. The conversations encouraged participants to take several practical steps towards living more sustainably; 77% said the exercise made them more aware of the environmental impact of daily life; 78% said it helped them reduce their carbon footprint; 66% were inspired to influence others in their social circle; 39% said that that experience helped them to reduce car travel; 35% said it helped them to fly less frequently. Some participants also reported feeling less anxious and helpless (Baudon & Jachens, 2021).

Eco-anxiety is an entirely reasonable response to a distressing situation that affects everyone. As with all forms of anxiety, attempts to reduce feelings of helplessness can be aided by forming links with like-minded people, in this case with a view to developing more sustainable travel options. Practical strategies for reducing eco-anxiety not only improve wellbeing; they may also encourage more people to travel sustainably.

Throughout this journey of the psychology of travel we have acknowledged the capacity travel has for lifting the mood (see Chapter 5), broadening the mind (see Chapter 2 and Chapter 6), forging relationships (see Chapter 2) and creating fond memories (see Chapter 6). We have also seen how it can elicit fear and anxiety (see Chapter 4), especially during times of uncertainty. The legacy of crises such as COVID-19 may be the coming of a new age of conservative travel, with norms and behaviours that adapt to cope with perceived risk. When these risks are perceived as being relatively low and fewer travel restrictions are in place, we may feel able to travel more hedonistically (see Chapter 5). The climate emergency presents a more fundamental challenge for travellers who care about the future of the planet. As we consider how to adapt journeys to the challenges of the future, it is likely that more people will develop more sustainable travel patterns, for example by avoiding unnecessary commuting, cutting down on long-haul flights, car-sharing, travelling more locally, cycling, driving vehicles that are powered more sustainably, taking fewer, longer holidays, rather than frequent, shorter ones, participating in holiday activities that benefit local, sustainable enterprises, avoiding single-use plastic bottles when on the move, carrying their own cup, asking hotels about water conservation, using fewer towels, teleconferencing, traveling overland . . .

FURTHER READING

CHAPTER 1: DEPARTURE: TOWARDS A PSYCHOLOGY OF TRAVEL

Bowles, P. (2000). *The Sheltering Sky*. New York: Ecco Press.

Bruder, J. (2020). *Nomadland*. London: Picador.

Cook, S. (2018). Geographies of mobility: A brief introduction Geography Vol. 103, Part 3 A: 137.

Dilek, E., & Dilek, N. (2018). The changing meaning of travel. *Tourism and Tourist Definitions, Conference*: 2018: VII. International Congress on Current Debates in Social Sciences.

Steinbeck, J. (2001). *Travels with Charley: In Search of America*. London; Penguin.

CHAPTER 2: DIRECTIONS OF TRAVEL: COGNITION, WAYFINDING AND HOW TO AVOID GETTING LOST

Cresswell, T. (2004). *Place: A Short Introduction*. London: Blackwell.

Golledge, R., & Garling, T. (2003). *Cognitive Maps and Urban Travel*. UC Berkele: University of California Transportation Center.

Ingold, T. (2011). *Being Alive: Essays on Movement, Knowledge and Description*. London, New York: Routledge.

Lynch, M. (1960). *Image of the City*. New York, NY: MIT.

Stevenson, A. (2017). Arrival stories: Using participatory, embodied, sensory ethnography to explore the making of an English city for newly arrived international students. *Journal of Contemporary Ethnography*, 46(5), 544–572.

CHAPTER 3: INFLUENCERS AND TRIP ADVISORS: THE SOCIAL PSYCHOLOGY OF TRAVEL

Ayeh, J. K., Au, N., & Law, R. (2013). 'Do we believe in TripAdvisor?' Examining credibility perceptions and online travelers' attitude toward using user-generated content. *Journal of Travel Research*, 52(4), 437–452.

de Certeau, M. (1984). *The Practice of Everyday Life* (Vol. 1). Minneapolis, MN: University of Minnesota Press. (Original work published 1974).

Fan, D. (2017). Tourist typology in social contact: An addition to existing theories. *Tourism Management*, 60, 357–336.

Oliveira, T., et al. (2020). Why do people share their travel experiences on social media? *Tourism Management*, 78, 104041.

Sun, N., Rau, P. P.-L., & Ma, L. (2014). Understanding lurkers in online communities: A literature review. *Computers in Human Behavior*, 38, 110–117.

CHAPTER 4: TRAVEL FEVER: A WORRYING WORLD OF FEAR, PHOBIA AND ANXIETY

Fennell, D. (2017). Towards a model of travel fear. *Annals of Tourism Research*, 66, 140–150.

Kahr, B. (2004). The psychodynamics of travel phobia: A contribution to clinical aerospace psychology. In R. Bor (Ed.), *Anxiety at 35,000 Feet, an Introduction to Clinical Aerospace Psychology*. London: Routledge.

Minnaert, L. (2014). Social tourism participation: The role of tourism experience and uncertainty. *Tourism Management*, 40, 282–289.

Monica Chien, P. (2017). Travelers' health risk perceptions and protective behavior: A psychological approach. *Journal of Travel Research*, 56(6), 744–759.

Zheng, D., et al. (2021). Afraid to travel after COVID-19? Self-protection, coping and resilience against pandemic 'travel fear'. *Tourism Management*, (83).

CHAPTER 5: HEDONISM AND SELF-IMPROVEMENT: HOW DOES TRAVEL MAKE US HAPPIER?

Argyle, M. (2002). The Psychology of Happiness (3rd ed.). London: Methuen.

Csikszentmihalyi, M. (1990). Flow: The Psychology of Optimal Experience. New York: HarperCollins.

De Botton, A. (2014). The Art of Travel. London: Penguin.

Filep, S., & Laing, J. (2019). Trend and directions in tourism and positive psychology. Journal of Travel Research, 58(3), 343–354.

Kay Smith, M., & Diekmann, A. (2017). Tourism and wellbeing. Annals of Tourism Research, 66, 1–13.

CHAPTER 6: UNFORGETTABLE JOURNEYS: NOSTALGIA, HOMESICKNESS AND OTHER TRAVEL MEMORIES

Howard, S. A. (2012). Nostalgia. Analysis, 72(4), 641–650.

Howes, D. (2005). Empire of the Senses. Oxford: Berg.

Morse, M., & Mudgett, J. (2017). Longing for landscape: Homesickness and place attachment among rural out-migrants in the 19th and 21st centuries. Journal of Rural Studies, 50, 95–103.

Rishbeth, C., & Powell, M. (2013). Place attachment and memory: Landscapes of belonging as experienced post-migration. Landscape Research, 38(2), 160–178.

Sedikides, C., Wildschut, T., Arndt, J., & Routledge, C. (2008). Nostalgia: Past, present, and future. Current Directions in Psychological Science, 17(5), 304–307.

CHAPTER 7: CULTURE SHOCKS AND BORDER CROSSINGS: TRAVEL AND INTERCULTURAL ENCOUNTER

Amit, V. (2015). Circumscribed cosmopolitanism: travel aspirations and experiences. Identities, 22(5), 551–568.

Berry, J. W. (2006). Acculturative stress. In P. T. P Wong & L. C. J. Wong (Eds.), Handbook of Multicultural Perspectives on Stress and Coping (pp. 287–298). Dallas, TX: Spring.

Ozer, S. (2017). Psychological theories of acculturation. The International Encyclopaedia of Intercultural Communication.

Rasmi, S., et al. (2014) 'Tourists' strategies: An acculturation approach. *Tourism Management*, 40, 311–320.

Skey, M. (2013). What does it mean to be cosmopolitan? An examination of the varying meaningfulness and commensurability of everyday 'cosmopolitan' practices. *Identities*, 20(3), 235–252.

CHAPTER 8: DETOUR: PSYCHOGEOGRAPHY AND THE ART OF SLOW TRAVEL

Antony, R., & Henry, J. (2005). *Lonely Planet Guide to Experimental Travel*. London: Lonely Planet.

Calle, S. (1998). *Suite Vénitienne / Please Follow Me*. Paris: Editions Acte Sud.

Coverley, M. (2006). *Psychogeography*. Harpenden: Pocket Essentials.

Solnit, R. (2014). *Wanderlust: A History of Walking*. London: Granta.

Stewart, L. (2022). *Walking Distance*. London: Avery Hill.

CHAPTER 9: WHERE DO WE GO FROM HERE? TRAVEL IN AN AGE OF ECO-ANXIETY

Hermann, I., & Morris Paris, C. (2020). Digital nomadism: The nexus of remote working and travel mobility. *Information Technology & Tourism*, 22, 329–334.

Hickman, C. (2020). We need to (find a way to) talk about . . . Eco-anxiety. *Journal of Social Work Practice*, 34(4), 411–424.

Makimoto, T., & Manners, D. (1997). *Digital Nomad*. New York: Wiley.

Reichenberger, I. (2018). Digital nomads: A quest for holistic freedom in work and leisure. *Annals of Leisure Research*, 21(3), 364–380.

Thunberg, G., et al. (2020). *Our House Is on Fire: Scenes of a Family and a Planet in Crisis*. New York, NY, USA: Penguin Random House.

REFERENCES

CHAPTER 1: DEPARTURE: TOWARDS A PSYCHOLOGY OF TRAVEL

Bowles, P. (2000). The Sheltering Sky. New York: Ecco Press.

Cook, S. (2018). Geographies of mobility: A brief introduction Geography Vol. 103, Part 3 A: 137.

Dilek, E., & Dilek, N. (2018). The changing meaning of travel. Tourism and Tourist Definitions, Conference: 2018: VII. International Congress on Current Debates in Social Sciences.

Hall, C., & Page, S. (2014). The Geography of Tourism and Recreation: Environment, Place and Space London. Routledge.

Hunt, J., & Layne, D. (1991). Evolution of travel and tourism terminology and definitions. Journal of Travel Research, 29(4), 7–11.

UNWTO. (2016) World Tourism Barometer 14 (6).

UNWTO. (2018). World Tourism Barometer 16 (5).

UNWTO. (2022). World Tourism Barometer 20 (4).

CHAPTER 2: DIRECTIONS OF TRAVEL: COGNITION, WAYFINDING AND HOW TO AVOID GETTING LOST

Allen, G. (1999). Spatial abilities, cognitive maps, and wayfinding-bases for individual differences in spatial cognition and behavior. In R. Golledge (Ed.),

Wayfinding Behavior: Cognitive Mapping and Other Spatial Processes (pp. 46–80). Baltimore: Johns Hopkins University Press.

Bonner, B., & Bolinger, A. (2013). Separating the confident from the correct: Leveraging member knowledge in groups to improve decision making and performance. *Organisational Behaviour and Human Decision Processing*, 122, 214–221.

Carpman, J., & Grant, M. (2016). *Design That Cares: Planning Health Facilities for Patients and Visitors*. San Francisco: Jossey-Bass.

Chang, H. (2013). Wayfinding strategies and tourist anxiety in unfamiliar destinations. *Tourism Geographies*, 15(3), 529–550.

Chang, K., et al. (2019). Tourist geographic literacy and its consequences. *Tourism Management Perspectives*, 29, 131–140.

Cresswell, T. (2004). *Place: A Short Introduction*. London: Blackwell.

Dalton, R. C., Hölscher, C., & Montello D. R. (2019). Wayfinding as a social activity. *Frontiers in Psychology*, 4(10), 142.

Downs, R., & Stea, D. (1973). Cognitive representations. In R. Downs & D. Stea (Eds.), *Image and Environment* (pp. 79–86). Chicago: Aldine.

Farr, A., et al. (2012). Wayfinding: A simple concept, a complex process. *Transport Reviews*, 32(6), 715–743.

Farr, A. C., Kleinschmidt, T., Johnson, S., Yarlagadda, P. K., & Mengersen, K. (2014). Investigating effective way finding in airports: A Bayesian network approach. *Transport*, 29(1), 90–99.

Fewings, R. (2001). Wayfinding and airport terminal design. *Journal of Navigation*, 54(2), 177–184.

Firth, R. (1936). *We, the Tikopia*. New York: American Book Co.

Forlizzi, J., et al. (2010). Where should I turn: Moving from individual to collaborative navigation strategies to inform the interaction design of future navigation systems. *Proceedings of the SIGCHI Conference on Human Factors in Computing Systems*, New York, NY: ACM, 1261–1270.

Foucault, M., & Sheridan, A. (1991). *Discipline and Punish: The Birth of the Prison*. London: Penguin.

Galton, F. (1907). The wisdom of crowds. *Nature*, 75, 450–451.

Gärling, T., & Golledge, R. (2000). Cognitive mapping and spatial decision-making. In R. Kitchin & S. Freundschuh (Eds.), *Cognitive Mapping: Past, Present and Future* (pp. 44–65). London & New York: Routledge.

Gartner, G., & Huang, H. (2012). Collective intelligence-based route recommendation for assisting pedestrian wayfinding in the era of web 2.0. *Journal of Location Based Services*, 6(1), 1–21.

Gibson, J. J. (1966). *The Senses Considered as Perceptual Systems*. Boston: Houghton Mifflin.

Gibson, J. J. (1979). *The Ecological Approach to Visual Perception*. Boston: Houghton.

Gladwin, T. (1974). *East Is a Big Bird: Navigation and Logic on Puluwat Atoll*. Harvard: Harvard University Press.

Golledge, R. G. (2002). Cognitive maps. In K. Kempf-Leonard (Ed.), *Encyclopedia of Social Measurement*, Submitted. San Diego, CA: Academic Press Inc.

Gregory, R. L. (1980). Perceptions as hypotheses. *Philosophical Transactions of the Royal Society of Biological Sciences*, 290(1038), 181–197.

Haldrup, M., & Larsen, J. (2006). Material cultures of tourism. *Leisure Studies*, 25(3), 275–289.

He, G., et al. (2015). Collaborative navigation in an unfamiliar environment with people having different spatial aptitudes. *Spatial Cognition and Computation*, 15, 285–307.

Hutchins, E. (2008). Cognitive ecology. *Topics in Cognitive Science*, 2(4), 705–715.

Ingold, T. (2011). *Being Alive: Essays on Movement, Knowledge and Description*. London and New York: Routledge.

Jamshidi, S., & Pati, D. (2021). A narrative review of theories of wayfinding within the interior environment. *HERD*, 14(1), 290–303.

Kitchin, R., & Blades, M. (2002). *The Cognition of Geographic Space*. London: Tauris.

Lin, C., et al. (2012). Gender differences in wayfinding in virtual environments with global or local landmarks. *Journal of Environmental Psychology*, 32(2), 89–96.

Lueg, C. P., & Bidwell, N. J. (2005). Berrypicking in the real world: A wayfinding perspective on information behavior research. *Proceedings of the American Society for Information Science and Technology*, 42(1).

Lynch, M. (1960). *Image of the City*. New York, NYC: MIT.

Malinowski, B. (1961). *Argonauts of the Western Pacific*. New York: Dutton.

Mark, D., & Frank, A. (Eds.). (1991). *Cognitive and Linguistic Aspects of Geographic Space*. Amsterdam: Kluwer Academic Publisher.

Massey, D. (2005). *For Space*. London: Sage.

McCullough, D., & Collins, R. (2018). Are we losing our way? Navigational aids, socio-sensory way-finding and the spatial awareness of young adults. *Area*, 51(3), 479–488.

Merleau-Ponty, M. (1963). *In Praise of Philosophy*. Evanston: Northwestern University Press.

Neisser, U. (1967). *Cognitive Psychology*. New York: Appleton-Century-Crofts.

Newell, A., & Simon, H A. (1972). *Human Problem Solving* (Vol. 104). London: Prentice-Hall.

Pati, D., et al. (2015). Identifying elements of the health care environment that contribute to wayfinding. *Health Environments Research & Design Journal*, 8(3), 44–67.

Pratt, M. (1992). Fieldwork in common places. In J. Clifford & G. Marcus (Eds.), *Writing Culture*. Berkeley: University of California Press.

Ruotolo, F., et al. (2018). Putting emotions in routes: The influence of emotionally laden landmarks on spatial memory. *Psychological Research*, (5), 1083–1095.

Spinney, J. (2006). A place of sense: A kinaesthetic ethnography of cyclists on Mont Ventoux. *Environment and Planning*, 709–732.

Stevenson, A. (2017). Arrival stories: Using participatory, embodied, sensory ethnography to explore the making of an English city for newly arrived international students. *Journal of Contemporary Ethnography*, 46(5), 544–572.

Symonds, P., Brown, D. H. K., & Lo Iacono, V. (2017). Exploring an absent presence: Wayfinding as an embodied sociocultural experience. *Sociological Research Online*, 22(1), 48–67.

Tolman, E. C. (1948). Cognitive maps in rats and men. *Psychological Review*, 55(4), 189–208.

Turner, S., & Leydon, J. (2012). Improving geographic literacy among first-year under-graduate students: Testing the effectiveness of online quizzes. *Journal of Geography*, 111, 54–66.

Tussyadiah, I. I. S. (2020). A review of research into automation in tourism: Launching the annals of tourism research curated collection on artificial intelligence robotics in tourism. *Annals of Tourism Research*, 81, 10288.

Urry, J. (2005). The complexity turn. *Theory, Culture and Society*, 22(5), 1–14.

Urry, J. (2007). *Mobilities*. Cambridge, UK and Malden, MA: Polity.

Vaez, S., et al. (2020). Visitors' wayfinding strategies and navigational aids in unfamiliar urban environment. *Tourism Geographies*, 22(4–5), 832–847.

Van Doesum, N., et al. (2013). Social mindfulness: Skill and will to navigate the social world. *Journal of Personality and Social Psychology*, 105, 86–103.

Xia, J., et al. (2008). The wayfinding process relationships between decision-making and landmark utility. *Tourism Management*, 29(3), 445–457.

CHAPTER 3: INFLUENCERS AND TRIP ADVISORS: A SOCIAL PSYCHOLOGY OF TRAVEL

Ajzen, I. (1991). The theory of planned behaviour. *Organizational Behavior and Human Decision Processes*, 50, 179–211.

Ajzen, I., & Fishbein, M. (1980). Understanding Attitudes and Predicting Social Behavior. Englewood Cliffs: Prentice-Hall.

Aldred, R. (2010). On the outside: Constructing cycling citizenship. Social & Cultural Geography, 11(1), 35e52.

Allport, G. W. (1979). The Nature of Prejudice. New York: Perseus Book Publishing.

Ap, J., & Crompton, J. L. (1993). Residents' strategies for responding to tourism impacts. Journal of Travel Research, 32(1), 47–50.

Asch, S. E. (1956). Studies of independence and conformity: I. A minority of one against a unanimous majority. Psychological Monographs: General and Applied, 70(9), 1–70.

Ayeh, J. K., Au, N., & Law, R. (2013). 'Do we believe in TripAdvisor?' Examining credibility perceptions and online travelers' attitude toward using user-generated content. Journal of Travel Research, 52(4), 437–452.

Bilgihan, A., et al. (2016). Consumer perception of knowledge-sharing in travel-related online social networks. Tourism Management, 52, 287–296.

Boğan, E., & Sarıışık, M. (2016). Yerel halkın turizm faaliyetlerine yönelik görüş ve algılamalarının belirlenmesi üzerine Alanya'da bir araştırma. Kastamonu Üniversitesi iktisadi ve idari bilimler fakültesi dergisi, (12), 325–342.

Bourdieu, P. (1984). La Distinction. London: Routledge.

Bowles, P. (1949). The Sheltering Sky. New York, NY: Penguin.

Brett, B. (2011). The psychology of sharing: Why people share online? New York Times Customer Insight Group, 1–46.

Brida, J. G., Osti, L., & Barquet, A. (2010). Segmenting resident perceptions towards tourism a cluster analysis with a multinomial logit model of a mountain community. International Journal of Tourism Research, 12(5), 591–602.

Çelik, S. (2019a). Social psychological effects of tourism Evaluation of the tourist-Local people Interaction within the context of Allport's intergroup contact theory. In D. Gursoy & R. Nunkoo (Eds.), Routledge Handbook of Tourism Impacts. London: Routledge.

Çelik, S. (2019b). Does tourism change tourist attitudes (prejudice and stereotype) towards local people? Journal of Tourism and Services, 10(18), 35–46.

Cohen, E. (1984). The sociology of tourism: Approaches, issues and findings. Annual Reviews in Anthropology, 10, 373e392.

de Certeau, M. (1984). The Practice of Everyday Life (Vol. 1). Minneapolis, MN: University of Minnesota Press. (Original work published 1974).

Dilek, S. E. (2016). Turist yerli etkileşimleri. In E. Duran & C. Aslan (Eds.), Turizmin Sosyal Psikolojisi (pp. 109–117). İstanbul: Paradigma.

Dovidio, J. F., Gaertner, S. L., Kawakami, K., & Hodson, G. (2002). Why can't we just get along? Interpersonal biases and interracial distrust. Cultural Diversity & Ethnic Minority Psychology, 8, 88–102.

Fan, D. (2017). Tourist typology in social contact: An addition to existing theories. Tourism Management, 60, 357–336.

Festinger, L. (1957). A Theory of Cognitive Dissonance. Stanford: Stanford University Press.

Fillieri, R., & McLeay, F. (2014). E-WOM and accommodation: An analysis of the factors that influence travelers' adoption of information from online reviews. Journal of Travel Research, 53(1), 44–57.

Fishbein, M. (1980). A theory of reasoned action: Some applications and implications. In H. Horve, Jr. (Ed.), Nebraska Symposium on Motivation (pp. 65–116). Lincoln, NE: University of Nebraska Press.

Gärling, T., & Axhausen, K. W. (2003). Introduction: Habitual travel choice. Transportation, 30, 1–11.

Guell, C., et al. (2012). Towards a differentiated understanding of active travel behaviour: Using social theory to explore everyday commuting. Social Science & Medicine, Elsevier, 75(1), 233–239.

Gursoy, D., & Nunkoo, R. (2019). Routledge Handbook of Tourism Impacts. London: Routledge.

Hsu, C. H. C., & Huang, S. (2012). An extension of the theory of planned behavior model for tourists. Journal of Hospitality & Tourism Research, 36(3), 390–417.

Kelman, H. C. (1958). Compliance, identification, and internalization: Three processes of attitude change. Journal of Conflict Resolution, 2(1), 51–60.

Kelman, H. C. (1974). Attitudes are alive and well and gainfully employed in the sphere of action. American Psychologist, 29(5), 310–324.

Kirillova, K., Lehto, X. R., & Cai, L. P. (2015). Volunteer tourism and intercultural sensitivity: The role of interaction with host communities. Journal of Travel & Tourism Marketing, 32(4), 382–400.

Maoz, D. (2010). Warming up peace: An encounter between Egyptian hosts and Israeli guests in Sinai. In O. Moufakkir (Ed.), Tourism, Progress and Peace (pp. 65–82). London: Wallingford.

Moufakkir, O. (2013). Culture shock, what culture shock? Conceptualizing culture unrest in intercultural tourism and assessing its effect on tourists' perceptions and travel propensity. Tourist Studies, 13(3), 322–340.

Munar, A. M., & Jacobsen, J. K. S. (2014). Motivations for sharing tourism experiences through social media. *Tourism Management*, 43, 46–54.

Nielsen. (2015). Global trust in advertising winning strategies for an evolving media landscape. *Nielsen Global Trust Advertising*, 1–22.

Oliveira, T., et al. (2020). Why do people share their travel experiences on social media? *Tourism Management*, 78, 104041.

Osatuyi, B. (2015). Is lurking an anxiety-masking strategy on social media sites? The effects of lurking and computer anxiety on explaining information privacy concern on social media platforms. *Computers in Human Behavior*, 49, 324–332.

Pernecky, T. (2015). Tourism, prejudice and societal conflict. In M. Lueck, J. Velvin, C. Eilzer, & B. Eisenstein (Eds.), *The Social Side of Tourism: The Interface between Tourism, Society, and the Environment* (pp. 11–38). Frankfurt, Germany: Peter Lang Verlag.

Pratt, S., & Liu, A. (2015). Does tourism really lead to peace? A global view. *International Journal of Tourism Research*, 18(1), 82–90.

Preece, J., Nonnecke, B., & Andrews, D. (2004). The top five reasons for lurking: Improving community experiences for everyone. *Computers in Human Behavior*, 20(2), 201–223.

Ronis, D. L., Yates, J. F., & Kirscht, J. P. (1989). Attitudes, decisions, and habits as determinants of repeated behaviour. In A. R. Pratkanis, S. J. Breckler, & A. G. Greenwald (Eds.), *Attitude Structure and Function* (pp. 213–239). Hillsdale, NJ: Lawrence Erlbaum.

Sedera, D., Lokuge, S., Atapattu, M., & Gretzel, U. (2017). Likes: The key to my happiness: The moderating effect of social influence on travel experience. *Information & Management*, 54(6), 825–836.

Sherif, M. (1966). *In Common Predicament*. Boston, MA: Houghton Mifflin.

Shu-Chuan, C., & Kim, J. (2018). The current state of knowledge on electronic word-of-mouth in advertising research. *International Journal of Advertising*, 37(1), 1–13.

Sirakaya-Turk, F., Nyaupane, G., & Uysal, M. (2014). Guests and hosts revisited: Prejudicial attitudes of guests toward the host population. *Journal of Travel Research*, 53(3), 336–352.

Sun, N., Rau, P. P.-L., & Ma, L. (2014). Understanding lurkers in online communities: A literature review. *Computers in Human Behavior*, 38, 110–117.

Tanford, S., & Montgomery, R. (2015). The effects of social influence and cognitive dissonance on travel purchase decisions. *Journal of Travel Research*, 54(5), 596–610.

Tomljenovic, R. (2010). Tourism and intercultural understanding or contact hypothesis revisited. In O. Moufakkir & I. Kelly (Eds.), *Tourism, Progress and Peace* (pp. 17–34). Wallingford: UK: CABI.

van Acker, V., Van Wee, B., & Witlox, F. (2010). When transport geography meets social psychology: Toward a conceptual model of travel behaviour. *Transport Reviews*, 30(2), 219–240.

Vermeulen, I. E., & Seegers, D. (2009). Tried and tested: The impact of online hotel reviews on consumer consideration. *Tourism Management*, 30(1), 123–127.

von Bergner, N. M., & Lohmann, M. (2013). Future challenges for global tourism: A delphi study. *Journal of Travel Research*. doi: 10.1177/0047287513506292

Yilmaz, S. S., & Taşçı, A. D. (2015). Circumstantial impact of contact on social distance. *Journal of Tourism & Cultural Change*, 13(2), 115–131.

Yoo, K. H., & Gretzel, U. (2008). What motivates consumers to write online travel reviews? *Information Technology & Tourism*, 10(4), 283–295.

Zhou, T. (2011). Understanding online community user participation: A social influence perspective. *Internet Research*, 21(1), 67–81.

CHAPTER 4: TRAVEL FEVER: A WORRYING WORLD OF FEAR, PHOBIA AND ANXIETY

Al-Tawfiq, J., et al. (2014). Travel implications of emerging coronaviruses: SARS and MERS-CoV. *Travel Medicine and Infectious Disease*, 12(5), 422–428.

American Psychiatric Association. (2013). *Diagnostic and Statistical Manual of Mental Disorders* (5th ed.). Washington, DC: American Psychiatric Association.

Asmundson, G., & Taylor, S. (2020). Coronaphobia: Fear and the 2019-nCoV outbreak. *Journal of Anxiety Disorders*, 70, 102–196.

Borger, J., et al. (2015). What are Europeans afraid of? *Guardian Newspaper*, 5 February.

Boss, S., et al. (2015). What do systems users have to fear? Using fear appeals to engender threats and fear that motivate protective security behaviors. *MIS Quarterly*, 39(4), 837–864.

Burkitt, I. (2014). *Emotions and Social Relations*. Los Angeles, CA: Sage Publications Ltd.

Chen, L., & Yang, X. (2019). Using EPPM to evaluate the effectiveness of fear appeal messages across different media outlets to increase the intention of breast self-examination among Chinese women. *Health Communication*, 34(11), 1369–1376.

Chien, P. M., Sharifpour, M., Ritchie, B. W., & Watson, B. (2017). Travelers' health risk perceptions and protective behavior: A psychological approach. *Journal of Travel Research*, 56(6), 744–759.

Choy, Y., et al. (2007). Treatment of specific phobia in adults. *Clinical Psychology Review*, 27, 266–286.

Cisler, J., et al. (2009). Disgust, fear, and the anxiety disorders: A critical review. *Clinical Psychology Review*, 29(1), 34–46.

Cohen, E., & Avieli, N. (2004). Food in tourism: Attraction and impediment. *Annals of Tourism Research*, 31(4), 755–778.

Cort, D. A., & King, M. (1979). Some correlates of culture shock among American tourists in Africa. *International Journal of Intercultural Relations*, 3, 211–225.

Dalrymple, K. E., Young, R., & Tully, M. (2016). 'Facts, not fear' negotiating uncertainty on social media during the 2014 Ebola crisis. *Science Communication*, 38(4), 442–467.

de Jongh, A., Holmshaw, M., Carswell, W., & van Wijk, A. (2011). Usefulness of a trauma-focused treatment approach for travel phobia. *Clinical Psychology and Psychotherapy*, 18(2), 124–37.

Eaton, W., Bienvenu, J., & Mikoyan, B. (2018). Specific phobias. *Lancet Psychiatry*, 5(8), 676–686.

Ehlers, A., Clark, D. M., Hackmann, A., McManus, F., & Fennell, M. (2005). Cognitive therapy for PTSD: Development and evaluation. *Behaviour Research and Therapy*, 43, 413–431.

Eichelberger, L. (2007). SARS and New York's Chinatown: The politics of risk and blame during an epidemic of fear. *Social Science & Medicine*, 65(6), 1284–1295.

Essau, C., et al. (2013). Psychopathological symptoms in two generations of the same family: A cross-cultural comparison. *Social Psychiatry Epidemiology*, 48(12), 2017–2026.

Faulkner, J., Schaller, M., & Park, J. L. (2004). Evolved disease-avoidance mechanisms and contemporary xenophobic attitudes. *Group Processes & Intergroup Relations*, 7(4), 333–353.

Fennell, D. (2017). Towards a model of travel fear. *Annals of Tourism Research*, 66, 140–150.

Fraley, R. C., & Shaver, P. R. (2000). Adult romantic attachment: Theoretical developments, emerging controversies, and unanswered questions. *Review of General Psychology*, 4, 132–154.

Handley, R. V., Salkovskis, P. M., & Ehlers, A. (2009). Treating clinically significant avoidance of public transport following the London bombings. *Behavioural and Cognitive Psychotherapy*, 37, 87–93.

Jonas, A., et al. (2011). Determinants of health risk perception among low-risk-taking tourists traveling to developing countries. *Journal of Travel Research*, 50(1), 87–99.

Kahr, B. (2004). The psychodynamics of travel phobia: A contribution to clinical aerospace psychology. In R. Bor (Ed.), *Anxiety at 35,000 Feet, an Introduction to Clinical Aerospace Psychology*. London: Routledge.

Kingsbury, P., et al. (2012). Narratives of emotion and anxiety in medial tourism: On State of the Heart and Larry's kidney. *Social & Cultural Geographies*, 13(4), 361–378.

Kock, F., Josiassen, A., Assaf, A. G., Karpen, I., & Farrelly, F. (2019). Tourism ethnocentrism and its effects on tourist and resident behavior. *Journal of Travel Research*, 58(3), 427–439.

Lee, S. A. (2020). Coronavirus anxiety scale: A brief mental health screener for COVID-19 related anxiety. *Death Studies*, 44(7), 393–401.

Lu, S., & Wei, J. (2019). Public's perceived overcrowding risk and their adoption of precautionary actions: A study of holiday travel in China. *Journal of Risk Research*, 22(7), 844–864.

McKercher, B., & Lui, S. I. (2013). The nine safeties: How inexperienced tourists manage the strangeness of China. *Journal of China Tourism Research*, 9, 381–394.

Minnaert, L. (2014). Social tourism participation: The role of tourism experience and uncertainty. *Tourism Management*, 40, 282–289.

Monica Chien, P. (2017). Travelers' health risk perceptions and protective behavior: A psychological approach. *Journal of Travel Research*, 56(6), 744–759.

Noble, L., et al. (2013). The impact of injection anxiety on education of travellers about common risks. *Journal of Travel Medicine*, 21(2), 86–91.

Novelli, M., et al. (2018). 'No Ebola . . . still doomed': The Ebola-induced tourism crisis. *Annals of Tourism Research*, 70, 76–87.

Page, S. (2004). Transport and tourism. In A. Lew (Ed.), *Companion to Tourism*. London: Wiley.

Reisinger, Y., & Manondo, F. (2005). Travel anxiety and intentions to travel internationally: Implications of travel risk perception. *Journal of Travel Research*, 43(3), 212–225.

Ruan, W., Kang, S., & Song, H. (2020). Applying protection motivation theory to understand international tourists' behavioural intentions under the threat of air pollution: A case of Beijing, China. *Current Issues in Tourism*, 1–15.

Savage, I. (2013). Comparing the fatality risks in United States transportation across modes and over time. *Research in Transportation Economics*, 43, 9–22.

Schiffman, L. G., Kanuk, L. L., & Hansen, H. (2012). *Consumer Behaviour: A European Outlook*. Harlow, New York: Pearson Financial Times/Prentice Hall.

Sharifpour, M., et al. (2014). Investigating the role of prior knowledge in tourist decision making: A structural equation model of risk perceptions and information search. *Journal of Travel Research*, 53(3), 307–322.

Shimazu, A., & Schaufeli, W. B. (2007). Does distraction facilitate problem-focused coping with job stress? A 1-year longitudinal study. *Journal of Behavioral Medicine*, 30(5), 423–434.

Sousa, C., & Bradley, F. (2006). Cultural distance and psychic distance: Two peas in a pod? *Journal of International Marketing*, 14(1), 49–70.

Steimer, T. (2002). The biology of fear and anxiety-related behaviours. *Dialogues in Clinical Neuroscience*, 4(3), 231–249.

Stone, P., & Sharpley, R. (2008). Consuming dark tourism: A thanatological perspective. *Annals of Tourism Research*, 35(2), 574–595.

Torgersen, S., Lygren, S., Oien, P. A., Skre, I., Onstad, S., Edvardsen, J., Tambs, K., & Kringlen, E. (2000). A twin study of personality disorders. *Comprehensive Psychiatry*, 41(6), 416–25.

Wang, I. M., & Ackerman, J. M. (2019). The infectiousness of crowds: Crowding experiences are amplified by pathogen threats *Personality and Social Psychology Bulletin*, 45(1), 120–132.

Watkins, E. (2008). Constructive and unconstructive repetitive thought. *Psychological Bulletin*, 134(2), 163–206.

Widmar, N., et al. (2017). The influence of health concern on travel plans with focus on the Zika virus in 2016. *Preventive Medicine Reports*, 6(June), 162–170.

Wilson, J., & Richards, G. (2008). Suspending reality: An exploration of enclaves and the backpacker experience. *Current issues in Tourism*, 11(2), 187–202.

Winch, G. (2014). *Emotional First Aid: Healing Rejection, Guilt, Failure, and Other Everyday Hurts*. New York, NY: Plume.

World Travel, & Tourism Council. (2018). *Impact of the Ebola Epidemic on Travel and Tourism*. Retrieved 25 February 2020, from www.wttc.org/-/media/files/reports/2018/impact of the-ebola-epidemic-on-travel-and-tourism.pdf

Zencker, S., et al. (2021). Too afraid to travel? Development of a Pandemic (COVID-19) Anxiety Travel Scale (PATS). *Tourism Management*, 84.

Zenker, S., & Kock, F. (2020). The coronavirus pandemic – A critical discussion of a tourism research agenda. *Tourism Management*, 81, 104–164.

Zheng, D., et al. (2021). Afraid to travel after COVID-19? Self-protection, coping and resilience against pandemic 'travel fear'. *Tourism Management*, (83).

CHAPTER 5: HEDONISM AND SELF-IMPROVEMENT: HOW DOES TRAVEL MAKE US HAPPIER?

Argyle, M. (2002). *The Psychology of Happiness* (3rd. ed.). London: Methuen.

Camus, A. (1995). *American Journals*. London: Spear Marlowe.

Carson, S. H., & Langer, E. J. (2006). Mindfulness and self-acceptance. *Journal of Rational-Emotive and Cognitive-Behavior Therapy*, 24(1), 29–43.

Chen, C., & Petrick, J. (2013). Health and wellness benefits of travel experiences: A literature review. *Journal of Travel Research*, 52(6), 709–719.

Csikszentmihalyi, M. (1982). *Beyond boredom and anxiety* (2nd ed.). San Francisco: Jossey Bass.

Csikszentmihalyi, M. (1990). *Flow: The psychology of optimal experience*. New York: HarperCollins.

Daniel, Y. (1996). Tourism dance performances: Authenticity and creativity. *Annals of Tourism Research*, 23, 780–797.

De Bloom, J., et al. (2017). Tourism and love: How do tourist experiences affect romantic relationships? In S. Filep, J. Laing, & M. Csikszentmihalyi (Eds.), *Positive Tourism* (pp. 35–53). London: Routledge.

De Botton, A. (2014). *The Art of Travel*. London: Penguin.

Filep, S. (2007). 'Flow', sightseeing, satisfaction and personal development: Exploring relationships via positive psychology. In *Proceedings of 2007 Council for Australian University Tourism and Hospitality Education (CAUTHE): Tourism Past Achievements, Future Challenges*, 11–14 February. Sydney, NSW: University of Technology, Sydney and the University of New South Wales.

Filep, S., & Laing, J. (2019). Trend and directions in tourism and positive psychology. *Journal of Travel Research*, 58(3), 343–354.

Fu, X., Tanyatanaboon, M., & Lehto, X. Y. (2015). Conceptualizing transformative guest experience at retreat centres. *International Journal of Hospitality Management*, 49, 83–92.

Garland, E. L., Geschwind, N., Peeters, F., & Wichers, M. (2015). Mindfulness training promotes upward spirals of positive affect and cognition: Multi-level and autoregressive latent trajectory modeling analyses. *Frontiers in Psychology*, 2(6), 15.

George, A. J., et al. (2021). Mindfulness-based eudemonic enhancement for well-being of individuals with alcohol-dependence: A pilot randomized controlled study. *Biomed Central Open Access Psychology*, 9, 116.

Jackson, S. A., & Eklund, R. C. (2004). *The Flow Scales Manual*. Morgantown, WV: Fitness Information Technology.

James, W. (1890). *The Principles of Psychology* (Vol. 1). New York, NY: Henry Holt and Co.

Kay Smith, M., & Diekmann, A. (2017). Tourism and wellbeing. *Annals of Tourism Research*, 66, 1–13.

Keogh, K. A., Zimbardo, P. G., & Boyd, J. N. (1999). Who's smoking, drinking and using drugs? Time perspective as a predictor of substance abuse. *Basic and Applied Psychology*, 21, 149–164.

Kirillova, K., & Lehto, X. (2015). An existential conceptualization of the vacation cycle. *Annals of Tourism Research*, 55, 110–123.

Laing, J., & Frost, W. (2017). Dark tourism and dark events: A journey to positive resolution and well-being. In S. Filep, J. Laing, & M. Csikszentmihalyi (Eds.), *Positive Tourism* (pp. 68–85). London: Routledge.

Levine, R. (1997). *A Geography of Time: The Temporal Adventures of a Social Psychologist, or How Every Culture Keeps Time Just a Little Bit Differently*. New York: Basic Books.

Maslow, A. H. (1954). *Motivation and Personality*. New York: Harper & Row.

Matteucci, X., & Filep, S. (2017). Eudaimonic tourist experiences: The case of flamenco. *Leisure Studies*, 36(1), 39–52.

Michalkó, G., Rátz, T., Hinek, M., & Tömöri, M. (2014). Shopping tourism in Hungary during the period of the economic crisis. *Tourism Economics*, 20(6), 1319–1336.

Mitas, O., Nawijn, J., & Jongsma, B. (2017). Between tourist, Tourism and happiness. In M. K. Smith & L. Puczko (Eds.), *The Routledge Handbook of Health Tourism* (pp. 47–64). London: Routledge.

Moscardo, G. (2009). Tourism and quality of life: Towards a more critical approach. *Tourism and Hospitality Research*, 9(2), 159–170.

Nawijn, J. (2011) Happiness through vacationing: Just a temporary boost or long-term benefits?. *Journal of Happiness Studies*, 12, 651–665.

Nawijn, J., De Bloom, J., & Geurts, S. (2013), Pre-vacation time: blessing or burden? *Leisure Sciences*, 35(1), 33–44.

Nawijn, J., & Filep, S. (2016). Two directions for future tourist well-being research. *Annals of Tourism Research*, 61, 221–223.

Packer, J. (2008). Beyond learning: Exploring visitors' perceptions of the value and benefits of museum experiences. *Curator: The Museum Journal*, 55(1), 33–54.

Packer, J., & Gill, C. (2017). Meaningful vacation experiences. In S. Filep, J. Laing, & M. Csikszentmihalyi (Eds.), *Positive Tourism* (pp. 19–34). London: Routledge.

Panchal, J. H. (2012). The Asian spa: A study of tourist motivations, "flow" and the benefits of spa experiences. *PhD Thesis*, James Cook University.

Pearce, P. L. (2005). *Tourist Behaviour: Themes and Conceptual Schemes.* Clevedon, UK: Channel View.

Pearce, P. L., Filep, S., & Ross, G. (2011). *Tourists, Tourism and the Good Life.* London: Routledge.

Pearce, P. L., & Foster, F. A. (2007). A 'university of travel': Backpacker learning. *Tourism Management, 28*(3), 720–740.

Peterson, C., & Seligman, M. (2004). *Character Strengths and Virtues: A Handbook and Classification.* New York: Oxford University Press.

Ryan, C. (1995). *Researching Tourist Satisfaction: Issues, Concepts, Problems.* New York: Routledge.

Ryan, R. M., & Deci, E. L. (2001). On happiness and human potentials: A review of research on hedonic and eudaimonic well-being. *Annual Review of Psychology, 52*, 141–166.

Schiffer, L. P., & Roberts, T. A. (2018). The paradox of happiness: Why are we not doing what makes us happy? *The Journal of Positive Psychology, 13*(3), 252–259.

Seligman, M. E. P. (2002). *Authentic Happiness: Using the New Positive Psychology to Realize Your Potential for Lasting Fulfillment.* New York: Free Press.

Tugade, M. M., & Fredrickson, B. L. (2004). Resilient individuals use positive emotions to bounce back from negative emotional experiences. *Journal of Personality and Social Psychology, 86*(2), 320–333.

Voelkl, J. E., & Ellis, G. D. (1998). Measuring flow experiences in daily life: An examination of the items used to measure challenge and skill. *Journal of Leisure Research, 30*(3), 380–389.

Voigt, C. (2010). Understanding wellness tourism: An analysis of benefits sought, health promoting behaviours and positive psychology well-being. *Unpublished PhD Thesis.* Adelaide, SA: University of South Australia.

Wu, C., & Liang, R. (2011). The relationship between white-water rafting experience formation and customer reaction: A flow theory perspective. *Tourism Management, 2*, 317–325.

Uysal, M., et al. (2016). Quality of life (QOL) and well-being research in tourism. *Tourism Management, 53*, 244–261.

Zimbardo, P. G. (2002). Time to take our time. *Psychology Today* (March/April), 62.

CHAPTER 6: UNFORGETTABLE JOURNEYS: NOSTALGIA, HOMESICKNESS AND OTHER TRAVEL MEMORIES

Altman, I., & Low, S. (1992). *Place Attachment*. New York: Plenum.

Atkinson, R. C., & Shiffrin, R. M. (1968). Human memory: A proposed system and its control processes. In K. W. Spence & J. T. Spence (Eds.), *The Psychology of Learning and Motivation* (Vol. 2, pp. 89–195). New York: Academic Press.

Baldwin, M., & Landau, M. J. (2014). Exploring nostalgia's influence on psychological growth. *Self and Identity*, 13(2), 162–177.

Barcus, H., & Brunn, S. (2010). Place elasticity: Exploring a new conceptualization of mobility and place attachment in rural America. *Geografiska Annaler: Series B, Human Geography*, 92, 281–295.

Barnes, S., et al. (2016). Remembered experiences and revisit intentions: A longitudinal study of safari park visitors. *Tourism Management*, 57, 286–294.

Bastiaansen, M., et al. (2019). Emotions as core building blocks of an experience. *International Journal of Contemporary Hospitality Management*, 31(2), 651–668.

Brockmeier, J. (2010). Remapping memory. *Culture & Psychology*, 16(5), 5–35.

Chaiklin, S., & Wengrower, H. (2009). *The Art and Science of Dance/Movement Therapy: Life Is Dance*. New York: Routledge.

Cohen, E. (1979). A phenomenology of tourist types. *Sociology*, 13, 179–201.

Cresswell, T. (2004). *Place: A Short Introduction*. London: Blackwell.

Diaz, X. (2007). An interactive sonic environment derived from commuters' memories of the soundscape: A case study of the London underground. Unpublished PhD. Thesis, University of Leicester.

Drever, J. (2002). Soundscape composition: The convergence of ethnography and acousmatic music. *Organised Sound*, 7(1), 21–27.

Eisner, E. W. (2004). *Memory Fitness. A Guide for Successful Aging*. New York: Verso.

Frochot, I., & Hughes, H. (2000). The development of a historic houses assessment scale. *Tourism Management*, 21(2), 157–167.

Frost, I. (1938). Homesickness and immigrant psychoses. *Journal of Mental Science*, 84, 801–847.

Hofer, J. (1688/1934). Medical dissertation on nostalgia. (C. K. Anspach, Trans.). *Bulletin of the History of Medicine*, 2, 376–391.

Howard, S. A. (2012). Nostalgia. *Analysis*, 72(4), 641–650.

Ingold, T. (2000). *The Perception of the Environment*. London: Routledge.

Järviluoma, H., et al. (2009). *Acoustic Environments in Change*. Tampere: University of Joensuu.

Kahneman, D. (2011). *Thinking, Fast and Slow*. Farrar, Straus and Giroux.

Kim, J.-H. (2010). Determining the factors affecting the memorable nature of travel experiences. *Journal of Travel & Tourism Marketing*, 27(8), 780–796.

Lee, J. (2004). Culture from the ground: Walking, movement and place making. *Paper at Association of Social Anthropologists Conference*, Durham.

Madoglou, A., et al. (2017). Representations of autobiographical nostalgic memories: Generational effect, gender, nostalgia proneness and communication of nostalgic experiences. *Journal of Integrated Social Sciences*, 7(1), 60–88.

Mankekar, P. (2002). India shopping; Indian grocery stores and transnational configuration of belonging. *Ethnos*, 67(1), 75–98.

Morgan, M., & Xu, F. (2009). Student travel experiences: Memories and dreams. *Journal of Hospitality, Marketing & Management*, 18, 216–236.

Morse, M., & Mudgett, J. (2017). Longing for landscape: Homesickness and place attachment among rural out-migrants in the 19th and 21st centuries. *Journal of Rural Studies*, 50, 95–103.

Odzakovic, E., et al. (2020). 'Overjoyed that I can go outside': Using walking interviews to learn about the lived experience and meaning of neighbourhood for people living with dementia. *Dementia*, 19(7), 2199–2219.

Prayag, G., & Lee, C. (2018). Tourist motivation and place attachment: The mediating effects of service interactions with hotel employees. *Journal of Travel & Tourism Marketing*, 36(1), 90–106.

Rishbeth, C., & Powell, M. (2013). Place attachment and memory: Landscapes of belonging as experienced post-migration. *Landscape Research*, 38(2), 160–178. doi:10.1080/01426397.2011.642344

Scannell, L., & Gifford, R. (2010). Defining place attachment: A tripartite organizing framework. *Journal of Environmental Psychology*, 30, 1–10.

Schine, J. (2010). Movement, memory & the senses in soundscape studies. *Sensory Studies*. Retrieved 17 June 2013, from www.sensorystudies.org/sensorial-investigations/movement-memory-the-senses-in-soundscape-studies

Sedikides, C., & Wildschut, T. (2018). Finding meaning in Nostalgia. *Review of General Psychology*, 22(1), 48–61.

Sedikides, C., Wildschut, T., Arndt, J., & Routledge, C. (2008). Nostalgia: Past, present, and future. *Current Directions in Psychological Science*, 17(5), 304–307.

Steg, L., & de Groot, J. (2018). *Environmental Psychology: An Introduction* (2nd ed.). John Wiley & Sons Ltd.

Steg, L., et al. (2013). *Environmental Psychology*. London: Wiley.

Steinbeck, J. (1960). *Travels with Charley*. London: Penguin.

Stevenson, A. (2014). We came here to remember: Using participatory sensory ethnography to explore memory as emplaced, embodied practice. *Qualitative Research in Psychology*, 11(4), 335–3.

Stylos, N., Vassiliadis, C. A., Bellou, V., & Andronikidis, A. (2016). Destination images, holistic images and personal normative beliefs: Predictors of intention to revisit a destination. *Tourism Management*, 53, 40–60.

Sutton, D. E. (2001). *Remembrance of Repasts: An Anthropology of Food and Memory*. Oxford, UK: Berg.

Thrift, N. (2008). *Non-Representational Theory*. Abingdon: Routledge.

Tod, D., Thatcher, J., & Rahman, R. (2010). *Sports Psychology*. Basingstoke: Palgrave.

Tsai, C.-T., Hsu, H., & Chen, C.-C. (2020). An examination of experiential quality, nostalgia, place attachment and behavioral intentions of hospitality customers. *Journal of Hospitality Marketing & Management*, 29(7), 869–885.

Urry, J. (1990). *The Tourist Gaze*. London: Sage.

Verplanken, B. (2012). When bittersweet turns sour: Adverse effects of nostalgia on habitual worriers. *European Journal of Social Psychology*, 42(3), 285–289.

Wang, N. (2000). *Tourism and Modernity: A Sociological Analysis*. Oxford, UK: Pergamon Press.

Ye, S., Ng, T., & Lam, C. (2017). Nostalgia and temporal life satisfaction. *Journal of Happiness Studies*, 19(6), 1749–1762.

Zhang, X., Chen, Z., & Jin, H. (2021). The effect of tourists' autobiographical memory on revisit intention: Does nostalgia promote revisiting? *Journal of Tourism Research*, 26(2), 147–166.

CHAPTER 7: CULTURE SHOCKS AND BORDER CROSSINGS: TRAVEL AND INTERCULTURAL ENCOUNTER

Amit, V. (2015). Circumscribed cosmopolitanism: Travel aspirations and experiences. *Identities*, 22(5), 551–568.

Beckstead, Z. (2010). Liminality in acculturation and pilgrimage: When movement becomes meaningful. *Culture & Psychology*, 16(3), 383–393.

Berno, T., & Ward, C. (2005). Innocence abroad: A pocket guide to psychological research on tourism. *American Psychologist*, 60(6), 593–600.

Berry, J. W. (2006). Acculturative stress. In P. T. P. Wong & L. C. J. Wong (Eds.), *Handbook of Multicultural Perspectives on Stress and Coping* (pp. 287–298). Dallas, TX: Spring.

Berry, J. W. (2017). Theories and models of acculturation. In S. J. Schwartz & J. Ungar (Eds.), *Oxford Handbook of Acculturation and Health* (pp. 15–28). Oxford: Oxford University Press.

Berry, J. W., et al. (2011). *Cross-Cultural Psychology: Research and Applications*. Cambridge: Cambridge University Press.

Bluic, A., et al. (2018). Enacting collective support for the European integration: Participation in pro-integration action and preference for specific trans-national acculturation strategies. *Journal of Community & Applied Social Psychology*, 28(1), 15–28.

Bruder, J. (2021). *Nomadland*. New York, NY: Swift.

Bur-Bayram, A. (2018). Nationalist cosmopolitanism: The psychology of cosmo-politanism, national identity, and going to war for the country. *Nations and Nationalism*, 25(3), 1–25.

Cleveland, M., & Balakrishnan, A. (2019). Appreciating vs venerating cultural outgroups. *International Marketing Review*, 36(3), 416–444.

Datta, A. (2009). Places of everyday cosmopolitanisms: East European construc-tion workers in London. *Environment and Planning*, 41(2), 353–370.

Delanty, G. (2006). The cosmopolitan imagination: Critical cosmopolitanism and social theory. *The British Journal of Sociology*, 57(1), 25–47.

De Leersnyder, D. (2017). Emotional acculturation: A first review. *Current Opinion in Psychology*, 17.

De Leersnyder, J., Mesquita, B., & Kim, H. S. (2011). Where do my emotions belong? A study of immigrants' emotional acculturation. *Personality and Social Psychology Bulletin*, April, 37(4), 451–463.

Eliassen, B.-M., Braaten, T., Melhus, M., Hansen, K. L., & Broderstad, A. R. (2012). Acculturation and self-rated health among Arctic indigenous peoples: A population-based cross-sectional study. *BMC Public Health*, 12, 948.

Gillespie, K., et al. (2010). Globalization, biculturalism and cosmopolitanism the acculturation status of Mexicans in upper management. *International Journal of Cross-Cultural Management*, 10(1), 37–53.

Graves, T. (1967). Psychological acculturation in a tri-ethnic community. *South-western Journal of Anthropology*, 23, 337–350.

Kwak, K. (2010). Self-development and relationships through acculturation. Culture & Psychology, 16(3), 365–381.

Lee, Y. T. (2010). Home versus host: Identifying with either, both, or neither? The relationship between dual cultural identities and intercultural effectiveness. International Journal of Cross-Cultural Management, 10, 55–76.

Lepp, A., & Gibson, H. (2003). Tourist roles, perceived risk and international tourism. Annals of Tourism Research, 30(3), 606–624.

Nguyen, A., & Benet-Martínez, V. (2013) Biculturalism and adjustment: A meta-analysis. Journal of Cross-Cultural Psychology, 44(1), 122–159.

Nshom, E., & Croucher, S. (2018). Acculturation preferences towards immigrants: Age and gender differences among Finnish adolescents. International Journal of Intercultural Relations, 65, 51–60.

Oikonomidoy, E., & Williams, G. (2013). Enriched or latent cosmopolitanism? Identity negotiations of female international students from Japan in the US. Discourse: Studies in the Cultural Politics of Education, 34(3), 380–393.

Ozer, S. (2017). Psychological theories of acculturation. The International Encyclopaedia of Intercultural Communication.

Panicacci, A., & Dewaele, J. M. (2017). 'A voice from elsewhere': Acculturation, personality and migrants' self-perceptions across languages and cultures. International Journal of Multilingualism, 14(4), 419–436.

Rasmi, S., et al. (2014). 'Tourists' strategies: An acculturation approach. Tourism Management, 40, 311–320.

Redfield, R., et al. (1936). Memorandum of the study of acculturation. American Anthropologist, 38, 149–152.

Rudmin, F. W. (2003). Critical history of the acculturation psychology of assimilation, separation, integration, and marginalization. Review of General Psychology, 7, 3–37.

Schwartz, S., et al. (2016). The Oxford Handbook of Acculturation and Health. Oxford: OUP.

Scruton, R. (Ed.). (2007). The Palgrave Macmillan Dictionary of Political Thought (3rd ed.). New York: Palgrave Macmillan.

Skey, M. (2013). What does it mean to be cosmopolitan? An examination of the varying meaningfulness and commensurability of everyday 'cosmopolitan' practices. Identities, 20(3), 235–252.

Sobre-Denton, M. (2011). The emergence of group cultures and its implications for cultural transition: A case study of an international student support group. International Journal of Intercultural Relations, 35(1), 79–91.

Stevenson, A. (2017). Arrival stories: Using participatory, embodied, sensory ethnography to explore the making of an English city for newly arrived international students. *Journal of Contemporary Ethnography*, 46(5), 544–572.

Stevenson, A. (2020). *Cultural Issues in Psychology*. London: Routledge.

Szerszynski, B., & Urry, J. (2002). Culture of cosmopolitanism. *The Sociological Review*, 50(4), 461–481.

Tajfel, H., & Turner, J. C. (1979). An integrative theory of intergroup conflict. In W. G. Austin & S. Worchel (Eds.), *The Social Psychology of Intergroup Relations* (pp. 33–47). Monterey, CA: Brooks/Cole.

Turner, V., & Turner, E. (1978). *Image and Pilgrimage in Christian Culture*. New York: Columbia University Press.

Ward, C., Fox, S., Wilson, J., Stuart, J., & Ku, L. (2010). Contextual influences on acculturation processes: The roles of family, community and society. *Psychological Studies*, 55, 26.

Yiannakis, A., & Gibson, H. (1992). Roles tourists play. *Annals of Tourism Research*, 19(2), 287–303.

Yu, Q., Pantea, P., & Gupta, S. (2019). Far apart yet close by: Social media and acculturation among international students in the UK. *Technological Forecasting and Social Change*, 145.

CHAPTER 8: DETOUR: PSYCHOGEOGRAPHY AND THE ART OF SLOW TRAVEL

Adams, M., & Bruce, N. (2008). Soundwalking as a methodology for understanding soundscapes. *Proceedings of the Institute of Acoustics*, 30(20), 552–558.

Alÿs, F., & Ferguson, R. (2019). Russell Ferguson in conversation with Francis Alÿs. In *Francis Alÿs: Revised and Expanded Edition (Phaidon Contemporary Artist Series)*. London: Phaidon Press.

Antony, R., & Henry, J. (2005). *Lonely Planet Guide to Experimental Travel*. London: Lonely Planet.

Bassett, K. (2004). Walking as an aesthetic practice and a critical tool: Some psychogeographic experiments. *Journal of Geography in Higher Education*, 28(3), 397–410.

Benjamin, W. (2009). *One-Way Street and Other Writings*. London: Penguin.

Bridger, A. (2010). Walking as a 'radicalized' critical psychological method? A review of academic, artistic and activist contributions to the study of social environments. *Social and Personality Psychology Compass*, 4(2), 131–139.

Budig, K., Diez, J., Conde, P., et al. (2018). Photovoice and empowerment: Evaluating the transformative potential of a participatory action research project. *BMC Public Health*, 18, 432.

Calle, S. (1998). *Suite Vénitienne / Please Follow Me*. Paris: Editions Acte Sud.

Corringham, V. (2008). *Skywalks, Playing with Words*. London: CRISAP\RGAP.

Coverley, M. (2006). *Psychogeography*. Harpenden: Pocket Essentials.

Debord, G. (1955). *Introduction to a Critique of Urban Geography*. Paris: Les Lèvres Nues.

Elkin, L. (2016). *Flâneuse: Women Walk the City*. London: Chatto & Windus.

Gallagher, M. (2015). Field recording and the sounding of spaces. *Environment and Planning D: Society and Space*, 33(3), 560–576.

Massey, D. (2005). *For Space*. London: Sage.

Moles, K. (2007). A walk in the third space. *Sociological Research Online*, 13(4), 2–4.

Morley, P. (2021). *From Manchester with Love*. London: Faber and Faber.

Pinder, D. (2005). *Visions of the City: Utopianism, Power and Politics in Twentieth Century Urbanism*. Edinburgh: Edinburgh University Press.

Rose, M. (2015). Confessions of an Anarcho-Flâneuse. In T. Richardson (Ed.), *Walking Inside Out: Contemporary British Psychogeography*. London: Rowman & Littlefield International.

Self, W. (2007). *Psychogeography*. London: Macmillan.

Sinclair, I. (2002). *London Orbital*. London: Penguin.

Solnit, R. (2014). *Wanderlust: A History of Walking*. London: Granta.

Spinney, J. (2009). Cycling the city: Movement, meaning and method. *Geography Compass*, 3(2), 817–835.

Stevenson, A., & Ordu, A. (2016). Abdication and arrival: Using an open ended, collaborator-led ethnography to explore constructions of newly encountered cities. In B. Campkin & G. Duijzings (Eds.), *Engaged Urbanism: Cities & Methodologies*. London: Bloomsbury.

Stewart, L. (2022). *Walking Distance*. London: Avery Hill.

Traux, B. (1978). *Handbook for Acoustic Ecology*. New York: A.R.C Publications.

CHAPTER 9: WHERE DO WE GO FROM HERE? TRAVEL IN AN AGE OF ECO-ANXIETY

Baudon, P., & Jachens, L. (2021). A scoping review of interventions for the treatment of eco-anxiety. *International Journal of Environmental Research and Public Health*, 18(18), 9636.

Blatt, K., & Gallagher, J. (2013). Mobile workforce: The rise of the mobilocracy. In P. Bruck & M. Rao (Eds.), *Global Mobile: Applications and Innovations for the Worldwide Mobile Ecosystem* (pp. 275–292). Medford: Information Today.

Büchs, M., et al. (2015). 'It helped me sort of face the end of the world': The role of emotions for third sector climate change engagement initiatives. *Environmental Values*, 24(5), 621–640.

Currall, S. C., & Judge, T. A. (1995). Measuring trust between organizational boundary role persons. *Organizational Behavior and Human Decision Processes*, 64(2), 151–170.

de Haas, M., Faber, R., & Hamersma, M. (2020). How COVID-19 and the Dutch 'intelligent lock-down' change activities, work and travel behaviour: Evidence from longitudinal data in the Netherlands. *Transport Research Interdisciplinary Perspectives*, 6, 100150.

de Vos, J. (2020). The effect of COVID-19 and subsequent social distancing on travel behavior. *Transport Research Interdisciplinary Perspectives*, 5, 100121.

Floyd, D., Prentice-Dunn, S., & Rogers, R. (2000). A meta-analysis of research on protection motivation theory. *Journal of Applied Social Psychology*, 30(2), 407–429.

Fraser, N. (2019). *Say What Happened: A Story of Documentaries*. London: Faber.

Glaesser, D., et al. (2017). Global travel patterns: An overview. *Journal of Travel Medicine*, 1–5.

Hermann, I., & Morris Paris, C. (2020). Digital nomadism: The nexus of remote working and travel mobility. *Information Technology & Tourism*, 22, 329–334.

Hickman, C. (2020). We need to (find a way to) talk about . . . Eco-anxiety. *Journal of Social Work Practice*, 34(4), 411–424.

Marin-Pantelescu, A., Tăchiciu, L., Căpușneanu, S., & Topor, D. I. (2019). Role of tour operators and travel agencies in promoting sustainable tourism. *Amfiteatru Economic*, 21(52), 654–669.

Masterson, V. (2022). How quickly is tourism recovering from COVID-19? *World Economic Forum*. www.weforum.org/agenda/2022/03/europe-tourism-has-slow-pandemic-recovery

Mkono, M. (2019). Eco-anxiety and the flight shaming movement: Implications for tourism. *Journal of Tourism Futures*, 6(3), 223–226.

Neuburger, L., & Egger, R. (2020). Travel risk perception and travel behaviour during the COVID-19 pandemic 2020: A case study of the DACH region. *Current Issues in Tourism*, 1–14.

Panu, P. (2020). Anxiety and the ecological crisis: An analysis of eco-anxiety and climate anxiety. *Sustainability*, 12, 7836.

Pikhala, P. (2019). *Climate Anxiety*. Helsinki, Finland: MIELI Mental Health Finland.

Pronello, C., & Gaborieau, J. (2018). Engaging in pro-environment travel behaviour research from a psycho-social perspective: A review of behavioural variables and theories. *Sustainability*, 10(7), 2412.

Punyatoya, P. (2019). Effects of cognitive and affective trust on online customer behavior. *Marketing Intelligence & Planning*, 37(1), 80–96.

Quintal, V., et al. (2021). Is the coast clear? Trust, risk-reducing behaviours and anxiety toward cruise travel in the wake of COVID-19. *Current Issues in Tourism*. doi:10.1080/13683500.2021.1880377

Reichenberger, I. (2018). Digital nomads: A quest for holistic freedom in work and leisure. *Annals of Leisure Research*, 21(3), 364–380.

Shamshiripour, A., et al. (2020). How is COVID-19 reshaping activity-travel behavior? Evidence from a comprehensive survey in Chicago. *Transportation Research Interdisciplinary Perspectives*, 7, 100216.

Sutherland. S., & Jarrahi, M. (2017). The gig economy and information infrastructure: The case of the digital nomad community. *Proceedings of ACM on Human Computer Interaction*, (1)1.

Tan, Y. (2020). Coronavirus: Are cruise ships really floating Petri dishes'? *BBC News*. www.bbc.com/news/world-

Thunberg, G., et al. (2020). *Our House Is on Fire: Scenes of a Family and a Planet in Crisis*. New York, NY, USA: Penguin Random House.

United Nations Environment Programme. (2021). *Annual Report*. www.unep.org/annualreport/2021/index.php

von Zumbusch, J., & Lalicic, L. (2020). The role of co-living spaces in digital nomads' wellbeing. *Information Technology Tourism*, 22, 2,

Wen, Z., Huimin, G., & Kavanaugh, R. R. (2005). The impacts of SARS on the consumer behaviour of Chinese domestic tourists. *Current Issues in Tourism*, 8(1), 22–38.

World Tourism Organization. (2011). *Tourism Towards 2030/Global Overview*. Madrid: United Nations.

Zheng, D., et al. (2019). Emotional responses toward tourism performing arts development: A comparison of urban and rural residents in China. *Tourism Management*, 70, 238–249.

Zheng, D., et al. (2021). Afraid to travel after COVID-19? Self-protection, coping and resilience against pandemic 'travel fear'. *Tourism Management*, 83, 104261.

INDEX

acculturation 5, 77–91
acculturative stress 79, 84
altruism 33
ambulation 95, 98
anxiety: coping with 44–48; eco 114–118; separation 43; travel 36–44, 49, 85, 110, 112
arrival 3, 4, 7, 8–10, 15, 18, 38, 60, 109, 111
art 6, 50, 54, 60, 93–96, 98, 100–102, 104–107
attachment: motivation 33; place 66–73; and separation anxiety 43
attitudes: and behaviour 22–24, 26–29, 116; changes in 29–30, 79–84, 87–91; and intergroup contact 2, 4, 12–15, 24–28, 29–31, 106–107

biculturalism 77, 84–85, 88–90

cabin crews 44
climate change 114–118
climate emergency 109–115, 118
cognitive behavioural therapy 47–48

cognitive dissonance 23, 116
cognitive mapping 10–12
commuting 1, 2, 24, 113, 118
compliance 30
conformity 4, 13
conservative travel 44–45, 118
contact hypothesis 28–29
coping with travel anxiety 44–48
cosmopolitanism 77, 88–91
COVID-19 39, 41, 42, 110, 111, 112, 118
creative research methods 53, 56, 100, 102
cross-cultural psychology 86
crowds 12, 14, 16, 21, 35, 38, 42
cultural: assimilation 81, 84, 85, 90; integration 81–84; marginalization 81–83
culture shock 38, 39, 45
cycling 22, 24, 71, 118

dangers of travel 28, 36, 38, 40, 111
dementia 72
Dérive, (drift) 94
digital nomads 113–114

disorientation 9, 94
doing the knowledge 71
Drift (*dérive*) 94

Ebola 41
eco-anxiety 115–118
embodied experience 16, 17, 19, 40, 41, 70, 71
epidemics 9, 41, 42, 110, 111, 112, 118
eudemonic wellbeing 50, 52, 54, 56, 60, 61
existential authenticity 64
experimental travel 97

Facebook 31
fear: of flying 42–44; of travel 36–48
fever, travel 37–40
flamenco dancing 54, 56
Flâneur 94–96, 100, 102, 104
Flâneuse 105, 106
flight: fear of 42–44; or fight responses 36; shaming 116–117
flow 51–59, 61
flying, fear of 42–44

gentrification 94
globalisation 89
global warming 114–118
group: cultural 29, 91; membership and travel behaviour 2, 4, 12–15, 24–28, 29–31, 106–107
Guernica 55
guidebooks 83, 97–98

happiness 49, 50, 51, 59–61
health and travel 2, 5, 9, 41, 45, 46, 49, 59, 60, 79, 85, 109, 110, 111, 112
hedonism and hedonistic wellbeing 50, 51, 58, 60, 61, 112
homesickness 65–67

host-visitor contact and conflict 26–30, 78, 79
humanistic psychology 5, 50, 58

identification 25, 30–33
immigrant psychosis 65
influencers, online 31–33, 51
intentions and behaviour 22–24, 42, 73, 116
intercultural encounter 77–84, 89–90
intergroup contact and attitudes 2, 4, 12–15, 24–28, 29–31, 106–107
internalisation 31, 33

liminality 53, 87
local travel 98, 112

maps, internal cognitive 10–12
melancholia 64, 66
memory: autobiographical 65, 73, 74; embodied 11, 69, 70–72, 75; emplaced 67, 68, 70–72; flashbulb 63; improvement and travel 64, 67, 69, 71; muscle 11, 70, 71, 75; olfactory 69; photographic 73–75; sensory 50, 66, 68; short and long-term 70; sonic 69; topographical 11
MERS (Middle East Respiratory Syndrome) 41
migration 5, 78, 82, 83, 88
mind-broadening travel 88–90, 118
mindfulness 47, 51–53, 55, 56–58, 61; social 14

navigation 9, 11, 13, 15, 16
nomads, digital 113–114
nostalgia 65–69

olfaction 69, 102

pandemics 19, 39, 41, 42, 110, 111, 112, 118

perambulation 95, 106
phenomenology 16–17
phobias 36–39, 48
photography 61, 66, 67, 73, 74, 95, 98, 100, 101, 102
physiological responses 37, 40
pilgrimage 2, 49, 87
place attachment 66–73
pleasure-seeking 50, 51, 58, 60, 61, 112
poetry 94, 95
post-traumatic stress disorder 47
prejudice 28
psychodynamic psychology 43
psychogeography 93–108

SARS (severe acute respiratory syndrome) 110
savouring the moment 60
self-efficacy 47
sensory experience 69, 71, 73, 100, 101, 102, 107
sensory memory 50, 66, 68
separation anxiety 43
situationism 94, 95
slow travel 94, 107
social distancing 111–113
social identity 24, 34
social influence 13, 21, 24, 30, 32, 116
social mindfulness 14
soundwalking 100, 101, 107
stress 23, 59; acculturative 79, 84
sustainability 44–45, 107, 113, 116, 117, 118–119

theory of planned behaviour 22
theory of reasoned action 22
theory of repeated behaviour 24
therapy: cognitive behavioural (CBT) 47–48; eco 117; memory and 72
tourism 9; acculturation and 78, 82, 83, 86; anti- 97, 98; anxiety, fear,
phobia and 37–41, 44; attitude change and 29–30; birth of 98; characteristics of 1–2; group dynamics and 27–29; host visitor contact and 27–29; influencers and 31–33, 51; memory and 66, 73
tourist gaze 74
travel: anxiety 36–44, 49, 85, 110, 112; broadens the mind 88–90, 118; conservative 44–45, 118; creative 97, 98; experimental 97; fear 36–44; fever 37–40; guidebooks 83, 97–98; hedonistic 50, 51, 58, 60, 61, 112; influencers 31–33, 51; memory 63–75; phobia 36–39, 48; photography 73–75; responsible 44–45, 118; slow 94, 107; sustainable 107, 113, 116, 117, 118–119; tourism versus 2
travel versus 2
trends in 2–3, 109–111; wellbeing and 53, 59
TripAdvisor 31–33, 51
types of travelers 25, 26

walking: ambulation 95, 98; art and 98–104; feminism and 104–107; interviews 100; memory and 70–73; perambulation 95, 106; psychogeography and 93–108; research method 94, 98; soundwalking 100, 101, 107; with turtles 96; wayfinding and 15, 17, 18; women and 104–107
wayfinding 7, 19
wellbeing: eudemonic 50, 52, 54, 56, 60, 61; flow and 51–59, 61; hedonistic 50, 51, 58, 60, 61, 112; mindfulness and 47, 51–53, 55, 56–58, 61
whitewater rafting 53, 54
worry 37, 38, 40, 46, 115

Printed in the United States
by Baker & Taylor Publisher Services